David Weinberg

Off-Broadway / Off-West End

American Influence on the Alternative Theatre Movement in Britain 1956–1980

The author would like to dedicate this book to Joan Schwitzer 1925–2009 and Mat Schwitzer 1917–2014.

David Weinberg

OFF-BROADWAY / OFF-WEST END

American Influence on the
Alternative Theatre Movement in Britain 1956–1980

ibidem-Verlag
Stuttgart

Bibliographic information published by the Deutsche Nationalbibliothek
Die Deutsche Nationalbibliothek lists this publication in the Deutsche Nationalbibliografie; detailed bibliographic data are available in the Internet at http://dnb.d-nb.de.

Bibliografische Information der Deutschen Nationalbibliothek
Die Deutsche Nationalbibliothek verzeichnet diese Publikation in der Deutschen Nationalbibliografie; detaillierte bibliografische Daten sind im Internet über http://dnb.d-nb.de abrufbar.

ISBN-13: 978-3-8382-1082-7

Printed in the United States of America

My sincere gratitude to Elizabeth Francis and Elsa De Jong who helped me to prepare the manuscript for publication.

Contents

Chapter One: Introduction and context

This book argues that American experimental theatre practice as it developed after World War II primarily in New York was one key factor in the development of an important phase in the history of the alternative theatre movement in Britain during the period 1956–1980. The data for this study has been collected through interviews, archival work, and a review of existing literature on post-war British theatre including the alternative theatre movement. The theoretical structure and modes of analysis build upon key concepts and theories in the work of Elizabeth Burns (1972) and Baz Kershaw (1992, 1999). The main historical developments or phenomena referred to are the activities of the experimental theatre groups associated with Jim Haynes, Charles Marowitz, Nancy Meckler, and Ed Berman, four expatriate American theatre practitioners living in Britain during the time period 1956–1980. In addition this study examines important American based groups, Living Theatre (1947), Open Theatre (1964), La MaMa (1960), and Bread and Puppet (1965), which performed in Britain and which made an impact during the same period. This book also addresses a wide range of indigenous British groups, Pip Simmons (1968), Foco Novo (1972–1989), Joint Stock (1974–1989), as well as institutions, RSC (1961), Royal Court (1956), and individuals such as Max Stafford-Clark, and in passing Thelma Holt, John Arden, and the Portable playwrights (1968–1972), which in one way or another were influenced by American exemplars. As Colin Chambers observes of developments following 1956,

> Significant early manifestations of this [American] influence included the 1967 visit of Café La MaMa and the Open Theatre; the opening the following year of the Arts Lab, which spawned the People Show, Pip Simmons, and the Freehold; Portable Theatre, and Marowitz's Open Space; Ed Berman's Inter-Action, and its Other Company (directed by Naftali Yavin), exploring

> new relationships between actor, director, and audience; the Traverse in Edinburgh, with its workshop offering a new involvement for writers; the different combinations of left-wing theatre—Unity, Centre 42, CAST, Red Ladder; women's theatre, black theatre, gay theatre, theatre-in-education, physical theatre, community theatre, lunchtime theatre, and so on. (Chambers 1980: 7–8)

This book examines the wider historiographical context as it examines the exchange of cultural and political ideology through theatre and performance as well as important cultural institutions. This study will contextualise American influence by addressing ideas that were revolutionising broader culture and draw a parallel between the practices and practitioners examined and theoretical movements which provided the intellectual force behind changes in theatrical strategies. The deconstruction of canonical texts, collectively authored theatre, and performance, and innovative approaches to text, language, and physicality will be discussed with reference to relevant cultural frameworks.

In presenting this study the lead-in material includes two chapters. The first chapter introduces a discussion of the core argument of the book and its implications and includes a map of the book, a brief methodology statement, and a description of the methods used throughout the project. The literature review has been integrated and is framed around the central research question. The core chapters of the book involve a combination of analytic and argumentative explanations derived from different components of the research. The final chapter then integrates conclusions drawn from the core chapters through analysis and discussion.

It is important to state clearly that this book does not claim that American experimental theatre and performance practices were the only influence on this important phase in the history of alternative theatre in Britain. There were other important theatrical influences including Brecht, as well as separately Ionesco, Genet,

Beckett, (what Martin Esslin categorised as the 'Theatre of the Absurd' in 1961). In his 1961 book Esslin suggests that theatre had a delayed reaction to movements which had changed other art forms earlier in the twentieth century such as abstract expressionism. American influence on the alternative theatre movement in Britain during this period should be considered as one aspect within a larger movement in British culture. There were also indigenous groups such as the Unity Theatres, Theatre Workshop with Joan Littlewood, and, in its early years Ewan McColl, and the network of groups described in Norman Marshall's book *The Other Theatre* (1947). This study simply claims that American experimental theatre groups and performance practices as well as prevailing themes had an impact on changing and developing performance conventions and subject material within the British alternative theatre 1956–1980 which has not thus far been fully acknowledged or examined by scholars. Such an examination will contribute to a more comprehensive and dynamic understanding of the forces which shaped the alternative theatre movement in Britain.

Jim Haynes, Charles Marowitz, Nancy Meckler, and Ed Berman became key figures in an important new phase in the development of the alternative theatre movement in Britain. The groups and people associated with these four individuals would serve to delineate the antithetical purpose of the alternative theatre movement and establish an engagement between this sector and the commercial theatre establishment which could be argued had dialectical characteristics. A synthesis of alternative and mainstream characteristics has emerged and influenced the British theatre as a whole into a more comprehensive level of engagement with British society. In this a somewhat more representative and comprehensive number of communities and voices find representation. One could go to the most commercial West End Theatre in the present day and identify characteristics, such as an increased emphasis on physicality and non-verbal expression, colour blind casting, or the irreverent deconstruction and decentring of canonical texts, and trace these characteristics back to the influence of the alternative theatre movement. A number of the interviewees for this study explicitly made the point that, as in several other societies, there is a tendency in Britain for mainstream theatre to draw direct influence from the alternative theatre.

Altered Practices, Performance Efficacies, and Contemporary Literary Theory

In a conventional proscenium arch actor/audience scenario the audience is a part of an active/passive relationship. In conventional narrative-text-character based theatre the reception of the performance will be optically and auditorily focused and selective with regard to the incidents and their narrative significance. The audience member will sit in a designated position which orientates in a certain direction. The seat is fixed to the floor and the lights are extinguished except for a specific area where the performance activity is located. The audience is expected to acquiesce in a level of subordination and passivity. Ultimately alternative theatre, as its label implies, seeks varieties of alternatives to such a rigid format.

This study has identified certain markers of American alternative theatre practice which have dramatically altered the expectations of conventional theatre in the UK as well as the US to this day. Those characteristics include a subversion of conventional narrative, the exploration of non-traditional time, experimentation with location and space, an emphasis on a diversity of voices, and new approaches to the physicalisation of performance. Alternative British theatre productions during the study period, and after, have adopted, variously, a 'Pass the hat' economy, experimentation with audience and stage configuration and relationship (Total Space), artistic experimentation with form and content, Post-Brechtian forms of political engagement, non-traditional venues and audiences (lunchtime theatre, buses), non-narrative and language based (physical theatre), use of American 'Method' techniques, anti-class based form and content, and the use of obscene language and nudity. In addition British alternative theatre included experimentation with language (physicalisation and obscenity), experimentation with form (performance art and one-acts), and a breaking down of traditional hierarchies in terms of the economics and process of production as well as the actor/audience relationship. Further it has explored issues of identity as expressed in theatre in ways which problematise and challenge perception of national identity in terms of any single overarching or homogenising categorisation.

Such changes in practice derived from pressures of the moment, including complex relationships among and between theatre practitioners, complex intellectual and artistic influences upon those practitioners, and changes in production possibilities. Marowitz, for example, read Artaud at a critical moment in his artistic development, responding to Artaud's principles in specific theatre contexts. The specific reading histories of Haynes, Meckler, and Berman are less clear, but it is important to recognise that all four of the practitioners studied in this book, like performers in the theatres they founded, were all subject to movements culturally available to them at the time. Changes in theatre practice studied here paralleled major discoveries and shifts in literary theory before and during the period 1956–1980. Alternative theatre practices model certain ideas articulated by post-formalist, structuralist, Marxist, deconstructionist, and post-colonialist theorists. All of these theories had ideological implications. Though systematic analysis of these phenomena have been beyond the scope of this book, and my research shows that the practitioners presented here did not 'read' literary theory systematically, it is useful to identify certain theoretical movements or arguments prevalent in the intellectual and academic culture of the time.

Marxist ideologies were present and publicly available during the early twentieth century in Britain and America. The call to reassess existing economic conditions in relation to the cultural superstructures they engendered and sustained, as well as the Marxist call to change the world, were clearly present at the level of contestation and assumption in the foundation of Women's, Gay, Black, and Age-related theatres during the period studied here. Such ideas had become 'natural' as a form of discourse, to some extent, for many of the playwrights and practitioners studied here.

Formalist claims were also clearly available in Britain, given the work of IA Richards and others in forming a text-focused drive to interpretation. Alternative theatre, it could be claimed, contested text-based theatre, countering in practice the claims formalist theorist in the Anglo-American tradition made. Alternative theatre deconstructed the text as primary to dramatic performance and relinquished fixed text in favour of collective creation of language. It could be said that alternative theatre 1956–1980 offered a critique of text-based analysis even as it advocated collective action intended to 'change the world', both concepts with antecedents in Marxist theory. Similarly, audience participation and broken barriers between actor and audience could be claimed to represent resistance to 'class' and resistance to existing cultural institutions by a formerly 'passive' set of spectators, the audience.

The practice of 'laying bare' and the use of unusual devices in theatrical performance and technique has roots in Brecht but also in continental formalism. The contingencies of production and performance valued by alternative American theatre and transmitted to British alternative theatre could be claimed to parallel notions of relativity, and the deconstruction of text as primary might be aligned with contemporaneous ideas of decentred text. Undermining assumptions about who an audience could be and what it did could lead to redefinitions of race, gender, and identity as subjects for theatre. Finally, collective construction of plays can be said to reveal an awareness of Roland Barthes' assertions about the 'death of the author'. The potential reference to Barthes is certainly appropriate to the study period, however the analyst has to be careful. For Barthes 'death of the author' included the idea that everything is 'always already written' and that writers recombine what others have thought and written before. Clearly that is not the case with alternative theatre which innovated, sometimes outrageously.

These possible parallels would form a valuable study in future but were beyond the scope of this book as planned and written.

Alternative Theatre and the Nature of Nationhood

> 'I had no idea that England was broke. I will go over there and make a couple of talks and take over the British Empire.' (Clarke 2008: 47)

These words were spoken by the American President Franklin D. Roosevelt in a private conversation with his Treasury Secretary Henry Morgenthau in August 1944 while preparing for the Quebec Conference, held the following month and attended by British Prime Minister Winston Churchill and Canadian Prime Minister Mackenzie King. While Roosevelt may have intended his comments on some level to be ironic and to remain private, nonetheless they remain revealing. Between 1942 and 1945, three million Americans passed through Great Britain. It was the largest ever encounter between Americans and the British people in history. At one point before the D-Day invasion Americans made up six percent of the resident population of Great Britain (Reynolds 1995: 431–433).

As late as the 1920s Britain had controlled a quarter of the world's territory and a quarter of its total population. However, primarily as a consequence of changes necessitated by World War II the British Empire was to a large extent dismantled. These changes can be formally dated from the Quebec Conference in September 1944 when the war time allies began to plan for a post-war scenario. For the British this would culminate in the loss of India and Palestine in 1947. The Commonwealth as it exists today was formulated in 1949 as a free association of equal and independent countries, in effect to replace the Empire, though the process of decolonisation took two more decades to be fulfilled (Clarke 2008: 505).

By the end of World War II the joint Gross Domestic Product of Europe had fallen by about twenty-five percent while the Gross National Product of the United States rose during the war years by over fifty percent in real terms (Clarke 2008: xiv). Britain was saddled with enormous war debt while America had avoided any damage to its mainland. Later during the 1950s America made up six percent of the world's population but was responsible for fifty percent of global manufacturing and industry. There was, post-war, a shift of political and economic power and cultural influence to the United States. Britain survived the war but the cost would ultimately lead to the loss of empire (Clarke 2008: 508–512). Britain's war debts were not fully repaid to the United States and Canada until the year 2006. The Cold War solidified the current arrangement of US military bases scattered throughout the United Kingdom.

Besides the fact that the Americans Jim Haynes and Charles Marowitz were living and working in Britain from 1956 onward another reason for marking the beginning of the main focus of this study from 1956 was that it could be argued that there was an important generational shift taking place within British theatre itself as well as within British culture and society more generally. Austerity in Britain officially ended in 1956 but paradoxically as some measure of prosperity began to return, colonial attachments continued to disintegrate. Throughout the 1950s and 1960s, this disintegration was arguably accelerated by dirty wars in Malaya, Kenya, Cyprus, and Aden in addition to the 1956 Suez crisis.

Young men who had all, unless medically unfit or on grounds of conscience, to complete up to two years of National Service in the armed forces were beginning to rebel against the social and cultural constraints their parents took for granted, while young people of both sexes were beginning to question the values of a wartime generation. Meanwhile, as part of this process of generational rebellion, on both sides of the Atlantic, a Rock n Roll generation was emerging whose music was influenced by American country and rhythm and blues music, both themselves emerging from cultures which ran counter to the hegemonic White Anglo-Saxon Protestant culture which up till this period dominated American (and British) society.

During the 1950s General Eisenhower, who embodied in many ways older attitudes, was elected to the US presidency twice and former soldiers who were now in their thirties applied the discipline and group ethos that was engrained during the War into civilian activities. Meanwhile the younger generation who had greater educational opportunities as well as fewer financial restrictions and arguably, as a consequence, a greater emphasis on individual fulfilment emerged as a characteristic of the new 'Baby Boom' generation which by the late 1950s was entering its teenage years. Teenagers began to assert their own identities and it was in part because of these contrasts and contributing factors that a generational clash grew on both sides of the Atlantic, in which many American influences, including what may be described as an emerging youth culture, played an influential role. In 1956, in Britain, for example more than eighty local councils banned screenings of the hit musical film *Rock Around the Clock* amid widespread fears it would foment teenage delinquency.

Political turbulence in the 1960s encouraged women to re-examine their status in American and British society. Initially their claims were generally ignored, not only by the establishment, but also by male-dominated hegemonic political organisations which constituted the 'Nation'. In the 1970s the women's movement provided a new discourse on gender and sexuality that interrogated the patriarchal norms in society. The contraceptive pill arrived in Britain in 1961 but it was not widely available for women outside of marriage until 1974. In 1963 in the United States Gloria Steinem, a freelance journalist, became a Playboy Bunny on an undercover assignment for *Show* magazine. She exposed low pay, sexual harassment, and racism. In 1966 the National Organisation for Women was created in the United States.

In Britain, women were made dependent economically as they were paid substantially less money and also needed a signature from their father or husband to gain credit. In 1968 women working at the Ford plant in Dagenham went on strike for equal pay. The Dagenham, England, strike led to the Equal Pay Act in 1970 which was followed in 1975 by the Sex Discrimination Act. In 1970 women organised a highly theatrical protest at the annual Miss World contest held in London that year. Importantly, the women's theatre groups which emerged out of Ed Berman's season of feminist plays gave a theatrical outlet and voice to this movement in Britain and furthermore many of the other theatre groups which were a part of the identity based theatre of the 1970s in Britain started with seasons produced by Ed Berman.

In 1960 British Prime Minister Harold Macmillan addressed the South African Parliament in Cape Town and stated, 'The wind of change is blowing through this continent. Whether we like it or not, this growth of national consciousness is a political fact' (Younge 2013: 12). Over the next three years Togo, Mali, Senegal, Zaire, Somalia, Benin, Niger, Burkina Faso, Ivory Coast, Chad, Central African Republic, Congo, Gabon, Nigeria, Mauritania, Sierra Leone, and Tanganyika all became independent, as did colonies in other parts of the world, like Jamaica. Successful anti-colonial movements in Africa and Asia also encouraged ethnic pride and stimulated separate cultural nationalist movements amongst African American, Chicano, and Native American populations.

Such groups used the theatre to write their histories in the face of historic misrepresentation, calling attention to the suffering that they had endured and the struggles in which they were engaged. They showed that the dominant discourse in America had served the purposes of certain privileged groups and had disenfranchised others. In the late 1960s many identity based groups produced work within and for their own communities. Example of this included the Black Revolutionary Theatre, Teatro Campesino, and the Vietnam Veterans against the War, significant groups that called for urgent social and political change and took their message to the American people. The Teatro Campesino created work that initially responded to the 1965 strike in California by the United Farmworkers and performed on a flatbed truck in the fields. The Vietnam Veterans Against the War mounted 'search and destroy' enactments in the streets and country roads of the American heartland to persuade the American public to abandon the war in Vietnam and recognise their responsibility for the actions that were being committed overseas in their name. The Black Revolutionary Theatre had cultural centres in Harlem and Newark, New Jersey, where they produced drama, often in the streets that reflected the Black Power movement and Black Nationalism. This work was introduced to the British theatrical landscape in 1970–1971 with Ed

Berman's Black and White Power Season of plays which then inspired Black British theatre groups and playwrights to launch their own projects.

Even before then, American events and theatre practices had had an influence on mainstream British theatre. The American involvement in Vietnam began on a covert basis in 1954 and lasted until the fall of Saigon on 30 April 1975. During this period there were several protest marches in Britain, many of which involved a certain level of theatricality and included such groups as Bread and Puppet. Peter Brook's production of the anti-Vietnam war play *US* at the Aldwych Theatre took place in 1966. During the rehearsal process for *US* Brook and the RSC consulted with both Susan Sontag and Joseph Chaikin (Chambers 2004: 155). The Off Off Broadway movement also had a direct influence on the founding of the Other Place and Warehouse spaces at the Royal Shakespeare Company (Chambers 1980).

More generally during the period 1956 to 1980 the group as opposed to the individual became the focus of organisations associated with what came to be known as alternative society. This trend was also reflected in the structure of alternative theatre organisations that emerged during this time period. It was demonstrated in their working process and also in the performance pieces which they produced. Instead of the method of the traditional theatre in which a playwright writes a script in isolation and then other artists produce it, a new method of working sought to create a method whereby the group itself developed the performance piece from an initial concept all the way to a public performance (Shank 1972: 4). This method of working which is often referred to as 'devised' work is now commonly taught in specifically designed courses in British drama schools and is also common practice in British alternative theatre. The system of theatre censorship in Britain and taxation combined with a lack of public subsidy led to a situation where theatrical output was somewhat restricted. American work, meanwhile, was not created with the intention of satisfying these conditions and over time had a role in changing the prevailing environment in Britain.

National Contexts of International Influences

In the sense that it was a theatre of ideas and social action and not strictly tied to the profit principle, the alternative theatre movement in Britain can be traced back to the 1890s and the British premiere productions of *A Doll's House* and *Ghosts* by Ibsen and the founding of the Independent Theatre Society by Jack Thomas Grein in 1891 (Davies 1987: 36). The establishment of the Independent Theatre Society was indicative of a Europe-wide trend against the commercial theatre establishment, and the stated aim of the Independent Theatre Society was, 'to give special performances of plays which have a literary and artistic rather than a commercial value' (Davies 1987: 36). The Independent Theatre Society lasted for six years and produced twenty-eight plays during this period. It was replaced in 1899 by The Stage Society. Following subsequent phases in the development of the British alternative theatre movement, such as the Unity theatre movement that began in the 1930s, an important new phase came to grow and flourish during the 1950s and 1960s, characterised by certain variables mainly in the areas of means of production, artistic innovation, and political activism. Alternative theatre and performance represented an attempt to reshape the perception of the nature of the nation and its theatre.

In the years after World War II an economic boom in the United States eventually created economic conditions during the 1950s which led to a need for an alternative to Broadway in order to cultivate experimentation, discover new voices, and test untried material which in the pre-war period would have been possible on Broadway (Aronson 2000: 4). By 1951 New York was the richest city in the world and an inflationary boom during the 1950s drove the costs of production on Broadway to unprecedented heights while at the same time Broadway's audiences were being lost to the cinema and to television (Bottoms 2004: 19). The increasingly severe economic imperatives of commercial Broadway Theatre meant that conventional producers were unwilling or unable to risk money on unfamiliar names and unconventional material so that full scale productions produced on Broadway of plays by unknown playwrights became very difficult.

In this context the Off Broadway sector emerged in Greenwich Village. Greenwich Village was also the place where the 'counter culture' started as a rebellion against 1950s conformity. *On the Road* by Jack Kerouac was written in 1951 (published 1957) and figures such as William Burroughs, Allen Ginsberg, Thelonious Monk, and Jackson Pollock, to name a few were revolutionising literature, music, and the visual arts. There were important distinctions between Off Broadway and Off Off Broadway but there was also a certain continuity. During the late 1950s and early 1960s Off Broadway theatres also became increasingly commercial and as a consequence young theatre artists and writers began to form (and perform) in tiny cafes and non-theatre spaces such as church basements, lofts, and living rooms. Most of these spaces were also located in Greenwich Village or in the East Village and became associated with the label Off Off Broadway.

The emergence of these non-theatre spaces coincided with the blossoming of the downtown arts scene. Poets, dancers, painters, musicians, and filmmakers were simultaneously experimenting with anti-narrative based art forms and means of collective creation in comparable ways. Julian Beck, the co-founder of the ground-breaking Living Theatre, for example, was himself an abstract expressionist painter of some renown. Together with his wife Judith Malina they saw the purpose of the Living Theatre was to introduce the new movements expressed in experimental dance, music, painting, and poetry into live theatre (Bottoms 2004: 25). There was a breaking of traditional art form boundaries in the earlier part of the century as exemplified by the artists involved with Gertrude Stein in Paris but the theatre itself experienced a delayed reaction to these changes (Esslin 1961).

When considering the overall influence of American experimental theatre and performance practices emerging from post-war New York on the British theatrical landscape from 1956 to 1980 the introduction of experimentation of this kind into contemporary theatre practice in line with developments in contemporaneous art, dance, music, and poetry is of primary significance. For example, the mixed media interventions known as 'Happenings' were part of a fundamental layer in the development of alternative theatre during the 1960s. In 1911 Boccioni used part of a wooden window frame in a piece of futurist sculpture, and ever since 1911 or 1912 when Braque or Picasso, depending on which source one follows, glued a piece of real material to a canvas and originated collage, actual elements have been incorporated into painting. The picture moved out into the real space of the room. As an environment the painting then took over the room and finally as a sort of, environment with action, became the alternative theatre form known as 'Happenings' based at the Reuben Gallery in New York (Kirby 1965: 22).

Many commentators describe the alternative theatre movement in Britain as emerging from an international 'counter culture' during the 1960s (Ansorge 1975, Itzin 1980, Kershaw 1992). This study attempts to avoid the hyperbole often associated with talk of an international 'counter culture' and clarifies through close examination the particular national origin of prevailing themes and practices. Many of the revolutionary practices which were introduced through the Arts Lab on Drury Lane and the Traverse by the American experimental theatre practitioners detailed in this study can be traced to Greenwich Village and the East Village in New York City and the Off Off Broadway movement which began to take shape during the 1950s and included such groups and venues as the Living Theatre, Open Theatre, La MaMa Troupe, Bread and Puppet, Cafe Cino, Theatre Genesis, and the Judson Poets' Theatre. There certainly were contemporaneous examples of European experimentalism in the theatre such as Grotowski, Fo, Lecoq, Muller, Barba, Kantor, and Brook. This study recognises their importance as substantial and will later reflect in particular on the place of Brook within the argument, but this book is concerned with an area of influence which up till now has received less attention than these European experimentalists although perhaps in some way has been more influential on general theatre practice.

There were also prevailing American political and social crises which were of primary significance during this period in the alternative theatre in Britain including the war in Vietnam and the Civil Rights movement, even to the exclusion of contemporaneous British social and political developments such as growing tension in Northern Ireland and the status of ethnic minorities and immigrant communities (Ansorge 1975: 22–37). 'Cultural' and 'ideological' transactions took place and were brought about through the rupturing of established norms and contexts which were facilitated by the anti-hierarchical use of space, interdisciplinary content, and inclusive modes of audience assemblage and participatory performance practices (Aronson 2000: 7).

On 21 December 1968 in an article entitled 'The "Arts Lab Explosion"' Irving Wardle wrote in *The Times* that he was pessimistic about the future of experimental theatre in England. The reason he gave was that he thought that experimental work was merely an extension of American underground theatre. He believed that experimental performance was entirely alien to England whereas America had a tradition of acting ensembles such as the Living Theatre and the Open Theatre. He claimed that England had nothing except the music-hall tradition to rely upon for improvisational techniques. Although Wardle's statement is Anglo-centric and he did not mention the work of Terence Gray, Joan Littlewood, and Ewan MacColl or the work of the Unity Theatres in London and Glasgow during the post-war period this sentiment was echoed by both Peter Brook and Charles Marowitz at different times. Originally they were actually considering basing the Royal Shakespeare Company Experimental Group in Paris because they both felt it would be a more fertile environment for experimental theatre. The improvisational techniques Wardle was referring to were indicative of post-Brechtian practice such as those of the Living Theatre as well as American derivatives of Stanislavski and, although there was experimental work included in the Edinburgh Festival programmes during the 1950s, there was no permanent year-round base for this category of performance before the establishment of the Traverse Theatre club in January 1963.

Starting in January 1963 with the opening of the Traverse and later the Drury Lane Arts Lab in August 1967 the experimental theatre practices which would later pervade the alternative theatre movement in Britain found seedbeds in which to flourish. However the Traverse and Arts Lab were by no means the only places where American experimental theatre practices intersected with the advent of this important new phase in the history of the alternative theatre movement in Britain. Experimental theatre almost by definition was limited to tiny and unrepresentative audiences. Nonetheless I argue that experimental theatre had a special place in the mix of interlinking subcultures which by the end of the 1970s had transformed the British theatrical landscape and that it had identifiable effects on subsequent social and cultural developments. The theatres, clubs, restaurants, pubs, and festivals in which the experimental work took place were important physical locations around which a particular subculture itself overlapped with several other subcultures (Marwick 1998: 341).

> For us the "spirit of the times" means off-off-Broadway, Grotowski, and the Becks, more than anything we can claim as our own. Anyone who knew the East Village scene five years ago will find nothing new in the British underground's cartoon-strip treatments of American myth, Civil Rights reworkings of Greek tragedy, and celebrations of group-audience togetherness at the expense of coherence and skill. To that extent, the British avant-garde is more institutionalised than the most hidebound rep. And its dependence on foreign example is apparent in the fact that its three originating impresarios were all American. Charles Marowitz, Jim Haynes, and Ed Berman (in order of arrival) each added a separate American strain to the British subculture. (Wardle 1971: 178)

This British subculture was originally known as underground theatre and later alternative theatre, experimental theatre, and fringe theatre (Marwick 1998: 355). For the sake of coherence this book refers to these groups altogether under the heading of alternative theatre. Peter Schumann, the founder of Bread and Puppet Theatre, declared in the early 1960s that 'The audience which doesn't go to the theatre is always the best audience.' (Brecht: 1988, 609) Similarly the young David Hare of the British Portable Theatre insisted in the early 1970s that, 'Our aggressiveness is immensely conscious. I suppose it stems from a basic contempt for people who go to the theatre.' (Davies 1987: 170)

Broadly speaking, the defining characteristic of 'alternative' theatre is that it is not designed to satisfy the profit principle and is on some level intended as an alternative to the commercial theatre establishment and status quo. However 'alternative' theatre also suggests certain changes in the configuration of the theatre or performance venue itself such as theatre in the open or in the round without a traditional proscenium arch dividing actors from audience. 'Traverse' is actually a derivation of 'Transverse' and it is worth noting that Stephen Joseph, who earned a degree at the University of Iowa, returned to Britain from the United States in 1955 and then, after developing his ideas first on tour and then at Stoke-on-Trent, started his theatre in the round in Scarborough because of his experience of experimentation with this stage configuration in the American theatre. In the UK it was after the Traverse Theatre club opened in January 1963 that the plethora of smaller studio theatres with modified stage configurations began to proliferate.

The most extreme experimental plays required a nonconventional setting but it was also possible for experimental plays to be put on in a traditional theatre as well. An interesting case in point is the Royal Court Theatre, a traditional theatre on a smaller scale some distance from London's West End. It was the site for many productions important to the general history of the alternative theatre in Britain including the days when it was still the Court Theatre and producing the works of Shaw and later in the 1950s producing Osborne's *Look Back in Anger* and the plays of Samuel Beckett. In the 1960s the Royal Court also opened the Theatre Upstairs which was a club theatre with a flexible audience and stage configuration. By concentrating on a range of theatres outside of the established metropolitan and commercial circuits we can trace the proliferation of experimental practices. It should be noted that sometimes plays from the most alternative of backgrounds ultimately ended up in the most established of theatre spaces.

During the 1960s several new American writers of promise had plays presented in London including Mart Crowley, Jules Feiffer, Jack Gelber, Arthur Kopit, Patty Chayefsky, Gore Vidal, and most notably Edward Albee. Gore Vidal's *The Visit to a Small Planet* was produced in London in 1960. Jack Gelber's brutally candid view of drug addicts in *The Connection* performed by the Living Theatre in 1961 had a run at the Duke of York's Theatre. In 1965 the Arts Theatre produced Jules Feiffer's *Crawling Arnold* for a brief run and the RSC presented *Little Murders* in 1967 and *God Bless* in 1968. Arthur Kopit's most important theatrical venture in London occurred in 1968 when the Royal Shakespeare Company presented the world premiere of *Indians* which ran in repertory for thirty-four performances. Paddy Chayefsky's *The Latent Heterosexual* was staged at the Aldwych Theatre in 1968 by the RSC. Crowley's study of New York homosexuals *The Boys in the Band* was produced in 1969 and ran for 396 performances at the Wyndham's Theatre.

Edward Albee was unlike most of the other playwrights in this group from the 1960s and was able to repeat his commercial success in London. His first Broadway play *Who's Afraid of Virginia Woolf* opened at the Globe Theatre in London in 1964 and won acclaim from the critics and ran for 489 performances. Albee's other Broadway works however were presented in repertory. The RSC produced *A Delicate Balance* in 1969, *Tiny Alice* in 1970, and *All Over* in 1972. Three of Albee's shorter works which established his reputation before he began to have productions on Broadway also had performances in smaller more experimental London Theatres. In 1960 the Arts Theatre produced *The Zoo Story* with *This Property is Condemned,* a one-act play by Tennessee Williams. *The Zoo Story* was revived in 1965 and appeared with Moliere's *George Dandin* at the Theatre Royal Stratford East. The Royal Court presented *The American Dream* and *The Death of Bessie Smith* on a double bill in 1961 for 423 performances. From the middle of the 1960s onward a new group of American playwrights like Edward Albee had works presented in Off Broadway theatres and these plays began to be produced in clubs and lunchtime venues and other small theatres in London. Plays by Ed Bullins, Michael McClure, and Jean Claude

Van Itallie appeared in London during the 1960s. During the 1970s Terrence McNally and Sam Shepard also stand out among this group of new experimental writers.

Intriguingly the alternative theatre of the 1960s and 1970s was profoundly influenced by the Americans with the interesting twist that American alternative theatre initially received far more acclaim in Europe than it did in the United States (Crespy 2003: 86–87). What was taking place during the 1960s and 1970s was a loose constellation of activities whose objectives at times were very different but, although there was never a singular unifying premise or manifesto, there was a shared antipathy to the conformity and commercialism of mainstream society and mainstream theatre. Creating a context in which theatre artists could truly be free to express themselves meant abandoning any adherence to the profit principle. When assessing the practices of these groups in material terms it is of great significance that many of them endeavoured not to charge money for tickets. In the first major *New York Times* article on the scene in 1965 it was described as the 'pass the hat circuit' (Bottoms 2004: 3). This also became a characteristic of many of the alternative theatre groups operating in Britain during the 1960s and 1970s, at least during the early phase of their respective histories (Marowitz 1990: 21).

Methodology

The book incorporates analysis of individual productions in tandem with the evolution of experimental groups which emerged during this period. Further, it establishes the background context of the exchange of American cultural and political ideology into British alternative theatre and performance with references dating back to the productions of American plays in the 1930s by left-wing theatre groups such as Unity Theatre. It analyses American influences on British Theatre with particular emphasis on the advent of an important phase in the history of the alternative theatre movement in Britain during the 1960s and 1970s. This book will seek to further elucidate the phenomenon of cultural and political ideological exchange by way of theatre and performance and trace its origins. Examining and contextualising this cultural exchange between Britain and the US provides an opportunity to explore and assess theatre and performance efficacy in shaping modes of cultural production.

'Performance efficacy' is a critical term for this book. 'Efficacy' has a range of possible meanings, practical, and theoretical. A performance is efficacious if it produces, induces, or provokes an effective 'transaction' (e.g. exchange) between performers and audience. 'Transaction' means that an audience participates in the performance event—both at the moment of performance and potentially thereafter as the audience remembers and enacts intentions brought to consciousness during performance. Forced to participate in the performance, audiences look afresh at social, political, religious, legal, and personal assumptions. The goal of participatory theatre is to effect change (Kershaw 1992: 257–258).

Context ('contextuality') determines 'performance efficacy': a successful radical production creates its own context which is immediate, momentary, and directed to the specific moment and audience of the production. Efficacious performances are also intertextual—actors adopt conventions, language, and gesture from the audience or presumed audience into the performance text, in certain cases spontaneously. Performances are localised, contingent, open, and dialogic, allowing for transactions cultural and ideological among audience, players, and text (Kershaw 1992: 257).

In the social sciences there are two main paradigms that form the basis of research. The question that divides the two is whether the methodology of the physical sciences can be applied to the study of social phenomena. The paradigm that is rooted in the physical sciences is called the systematic, scientific, or positivist approach. The other paradigm is referred to as the qualitative, ethnographic, ecological, or naturalistic approach. Each approach has developed its own values, terminology, methods, and techniques to understand social phenomena and since the 1960s there has been recognition that both paradigms have their place (Kumar 2005: 13). The qualitative mode of enquiry for this book is determined by the research purpose.

The period 1956 to 1980 was selected for two main reasons. Firstly, it was the time period in which all the individuals and groups discussed in this study were living and working in the UK. Secondly, this period coincided with a cluster of important and relevant cultural and political developments both in Britain and elsewhere which will be clearly detailed throughout this book. In the first instance this book seeks to establish the existence of an interrelationship between American experimental theatre and performance practices and the evolution of conventions of performance in the British alternative theatre between 1956 and 1980. Thereafter this study attempts to clarify why and how this interrelationship came into being and explore how these changes influenced British culture, identity, and society.

In reviewing the literature it soon became clear that the topic under investigation had roots in a number of theories that have already been developed from a number of different perspectives. The information obtained from different books and articles such as *Theatricality* (Burns 1972), *Stages in the Revolution* (Itzin 1980), and *The Politics of Performance* (Kershaw 1992) needed to be sorted with the main themes and theories in mind. It was important to highlight both agreements and disagreements among the relevant authors and then identify any gaps and unanswered questions. The existing literature deals with a number of aspects that have both a direct and indirect bearing on the research topic. These aspects were used as a basis for developing this book's theoretical framework.

For example Baz Kershaw (*The Politics of Performance* 1992, *The Radical in Performance*1999) identifies and explores the transmission of radical ideology through the alternative and community theatre movements of the late 1960s and 1970s by tracing the evolution of this theatre movement and its larger impact on British society. Kershaw along with others including (Ansorge 1975, Itzin 1980, Craig ed. 1980) identify the short lived Drury Lane Arts Lab (1967–1969) as the birthplace of the alternative theatre movement in Britain (Kershaw 1992:100). Kershaw's work is important for this study because he succeeds in creating a theoretical framework for describing, analysing, and questioning the ability of experimental British theatre to achieve 'performance efficacy' thereby providing an example for this study to build on. His work is detailed, original, and important, but it does not take into account American influences on British theatre during this critical period and even dating back to the origins of the Unity Theatre, influences which need to be identified and assessed if Kershaw's analysis is to be sustained.

Kershaw describes the alternative theatre movement as part of a larger contemporaneous 'counter culture'. For Kershaw, three characteristics of a new commitment to 'counter-culture values' and to radical ideology are visible in, and outcomes of, alternative theatre productions: (a) the decentring of the written text as the chief source of communicative signs in production, (b) performance event as an experience of participatory democracy, and (c) theatre as a radical response to the hegemony of the Western status quo. However, it is also possible to show that the advent of the alternative theatre movement was influenced by overriding crises and trends with a particular national identity.

> During the first three years of the English fringe movement the war in Vietnam figured more obsessively than did the increasingly explosive situation in Northern Ireland. Student protest seemed to be the prerogative of the Sorbonne and Berkeley rather than of Oxbridge. Racial tensions in US cities were more in evidence than were the problems faced by West Indians or Asians in having to settle in England. (Ansorge 1975: 23)

Kershaw describes the difficulty in accurately assessing the theatrical event and its impact on the subsequent behaviour of an audience. He discusses previous attempts to do so and addresses the difficulty in achieving conclusiveness and develops a methodological framework for analysing performance efficacy which is more theoretically and factually convincing.

> What if we pay more attention to the *conditions* of performance that are *most likely* to produce an efficacious result? And what if we broaden the canvas for analysis beyond the individual or production (but still including it) in order to consider theatrical movements in relation to local and national cultural change? (Kershaw 1992: 3)

Kershaw defines performance as an ideological transaction insofar as spectators are actively engaged in the construction of meaning as the performance proceeds. The 'transaction' is the continuous negotiation between performers and audience, company and community to establish the significance of the signs and conventions through which they interact (Kershaw 1992: 257). If there is an ideological transaction at the heart of a performance event and the spectator is actively engaged in the construction of meaning as the performance proceeds, then we must not only examine the theatrical event itself but the entire ritual in its totality. This includes both the 'gathering phase' as well as the 'dispersal phase' of the performance. We must examine both the individual instance of performance as well as the collection of practices. Kershaw's stress on alternative and community theatre as a mode of cultural production was intended to reassert theatre's underlying coherence as a cultural movement (Kershaw 1992: 10). Kershaw adopts a notion of culture as a 'signifying system'. By this he means a system of signs by which groups, communities, organisations, and institutions recognise and communicate with each other in the process of becoming more or less influential formations within society. 'Culture' is the medium which can unite a range of different groups and communities in a common project in order to make them into an ideological force operating for or against the status quo. (Kershaw 1992: 36)

> If I could demonstrate the ways in which the potential efficacy of particular shows related to the possible general efficacy of the movement, this might produce a convincing case for the impact of alternative theatre on British social and political history. Very few studies of this kind have been undertaken for any theatrical movement, and certainly the job has not been done for British alternative theatre. (Kershaw, 1992: 4)

Kershaw's work has been useful in helping to define the limits of this study. He is able to talk in terms of culture and society with reference to alternative and community theatre. It is important to note that his work is grounded in theoretical movements (Marxist/Structuralist/Formalist) which provide the context for changes in approach to text and language. This book endeavours to contribute an additional perspective regarding the potential efficacy of this part of British culture and society. Throughout this book specific publications are examined as well as the overall contribution of particular scholars, critics, and practitioners, whose work has helped to define, shape, and spread the understanding, reception, and practice of American influence on alternative theatre and performance in Britain.

This book is based on the hypothesis that experimental theatre and performance practices, primarily developed in Off Off Broadway theatres in Greenwich Village in New York during the post-war period, were exchanged with the British alternative theatre during the period 1956 to 1980 and had the effect of altering conventions of performance. A detailed exploration of American influence on the alternative theatre movement in Britain 1956 to 1980 will provide an important new perspective in understanding contemporary British theatre and performance theory and practice.

Procedures

Having identified what the study is about the next question was regarding how to go about conducting the study? What procedures would be effective in obtaining answers to research related questions? How to carry out the tasks needed to complete the different components of the research process? What should be done and what should not be done in the process of undertaking this study? Identifying the answers to these questions constituted the core of the research design for this book. The research design for this book is a procedural plan that was adapted to answer questions as validly, dispassionately, and accurately as possible within the framework of critical study. In order to create the research design for this book it was necessary to arrange conditions for the collection and analysis of data in a manner that aimed to combine relevance to the research purpose with economy of procedure.

The essential components of the methodology were face–to-face interviews, archival work, and a comprehensive review of all relevant journal articles and publications. To the extent that this study relies upon interview material it is germane to acknowledge certain inherent pitfalls in the process, and to outline how any potential problems with this approach have been mitigated. The interviewer needs to take into account issues regarding memory and recollection, self-mythologising on the part of the interviewee and the position of the interviewer in assessing the validity of the interview material. For example my personal association with the late Charles Marowitz pre-dated this study by fifteen years and so a process of triangulation with regard to examining specific events was employed. This included checking historical texts and newspapers with respect to facts reported during the interview, as well as comparing and contrasting as many reputable sources of information as were available. It is also germane to mention that because this book examines hitherto neglected contributions to British alternative theatre, in certain cases the interview material represents singular insight. I tape-recorded several hours of interviews with Jim Haynes, Nancy Meckler, Richard Demarco C.B.E., and Charles Marowitz. I met with Nancy Meckler and Richard Demarco, each multiple times, and accessed their archives. I also established a link with the Unfinished Histories Project run by Dr. Susan Croft, the official Inter-Action historian. Unfinished Histories possesses a catalogue of interviews and archive material pertaining to the alternative theatre in Britain.

Richard Demarco for example was co-founder with Jim Haynes of the Traverse Theatre in Edinburgh in 1963 and served as its Vice-Chairman from 1963 to 1967. During the interview Demarco described how the Traverse Theatre was intended as a permanent year-round home for the kind of experimental work that was taking place during the Edinburgh Fringe Festival for three weeks in August every year. He described how Ellen Stewart of La MaMa was in communication with him during the early months of the Traverse Theatre and was an important inspirational force in sustaining what was then an uncertain initiative. He also described the comparable material basis on which both the Traverse and La MaMa survived in the early years. In the case of the Traverse it was Demarco himself, who, with others, helped to sustain the venture out of his own pocket, in his case from his wages as a teacher and from the proceeds from of his art work which was put on display and on sale in the Traverse cafe. In the case of La MaMa Ellen Stewart fulfilled precisely the same function, supporting the theatre through her work as a fashion designer. Demarco was also important to British avant-garde theatre apart from his work with Haynes and was responsible for bringing Tadeusz Kantor and his company Cricot 2 to Britain for the first time in 1972.

Having completed these interviews I then devised the following outline for the book:

Chapter One: Introduction

In examining the alternative theatre movement previous commentators have not addressed the concurrent effect of American theatre and performance on radical and conventional British theatre during the time period of their analysis. This book seeks to address that gap and asks how American experimental theatre practices intersect and interact mutually with issues of performance efficacy with respect to the advent of an important phase in the history of the alternative theatre movement in Britain. Chapter One introduces the main topic and places it within the context of contemporaneous theoretical movements and changes in broader culture. In addition, indicators of American influence on the alternative theatre movement in Britain 1956–1980 are identified and discussed. This chapter provides a map of the book so that readers can more easily navigate each section. It also provides a methodology, and a set of claims about substantive and theoretical issues at the core of the book's argument. In addition, indicators of American influence on the alternative theatre movement in Britain 1956–1980 are identified and discussed.

Chapter Two: Background 1936–1956

The first production at Unity Theatre was a double bill of American plays which opened on 17 April 1936 at the Britannia Street Theatre in London. The plays were *Private Hicks* written in 1935 by Albert Maltz and *Waiting for Lefty* also written in 1935 by

Clifford Odets. The members of Unity obtained their scripts for these plays from an American magazine called *New Theater*. The Roosevelt government initiated the Federal Theatre Project in 1935 and many of the original productions the London Unity Theatre produced were originally developed as a consequence of the Federal Theatre Project in the United States and the Living Newspaper (Chambers 1989: 77).

Between 1942 and 1945 three million Americans passed through Great Britain. At one point before the D-Day invasion Americans made up six-percent of the resident population of Great Britain (Reynolds 1995: 431–433). American influence on British cultural institutions was substantial and long lasting. Following the war a new generation of 'serious' American drama started to enter Britain such as the 1949 London premiere of *A Streetcar Named Desire* by Tennessee Williams. In 1956 the New Watergate Theatre Club presented a season including *Cat On a Hot Tin Roof* (Williams), *Tea & Sympathy* (Anderson), and *A View From the Bridge* (Miller) to challenge the system of theatre censorship in Britain. Unlike plays written in the UK these plays were not written under the stricture of satisfying the British licensing provision.

Chapter Three: American Groups

During the period 1956 to 1980 the group as opposed to the individual became the focus of many organisations associated with what came to be known as alternative society. The rise of the commune movement in the 1960s was an example of this trend which was also reflected in the structure of alternative theatre organisations that emerged during this time period. It was demonstrated in their working process and in the performance pieces which they produced. The idea of a collective creation free of conventional and traditional hierarchical structures became the basis for a new method of conceiving and developing theatre and performance.

To a certain degree this was a reaction to what was perceived as a fragmentation within established society and established theatre, fragmentation perceived to be based on competition and arbitrary concerns (Shank 1972: 3). A focus on group living and group activities, including theatre, was based on the premise that individuals are capable of cooperation and that it is possible to establish a sense of wholeness through collective creation. The most important pioneering groups were the Living Theatre (1946), Cafe La MaMa (1961), the Open Theatre (1963), the Bread and Puppet Theatre (1963), Richard Schechner's Performance Group (1968), the Manhattan Project (1968), the Theatre of the Ridiculous (1965), and the San Francisco Mime Troupe (1959). There were also parallel UK examples, for instance the foundation of the Traverse Workshop Company in 1970 by Max Stafford-Clark, under the influence of La MaMa, who lived communally in the old Traverse James Court building in their first years of operation. The Traverse Workshop Company eventually evolved into Joint Stock (1974).

Chapter Four: Jim Haynes

Jim Haynes arrived in the UK from Louisiana in 1956 and became an instrumental figure in the founding of the Traverse Theatre in Edinburgh in 1963. In 1967 he started the Arts Lab on Drury Lane. These experimental venues were immensely important catalysts for change and innovation on both technical and aesthetic levels. During the same year the Traverse opened, Jim Haynes, John Calder, and Kenneth Tynan organised the Edinburgh Drama Conference during which one hundred and twenty of the most renowned playwrights, directors, and actors converged on Edinburgh. Attenders included Eugene Ionesco, Harold Pinter, Laurence Olivier, Peter Brook, and Edward Albee. The conference may be seen as marking the point when the experimental practices of the Edinburgh Fringe began to proliferate more widely to the rest of the UK. Haynes started the *International Times* on 14 October 1966 at The Roundhouse in Chalk Farm, London (Haynes 1984). Ten years after the founding of the original Drury Lane Arts Lab in 1967, 170 multimedia communities based Arts Labs were scattered throughout Great Britain (Lane 1978: 152).

Chapter Five: Charles Marowitz

Charles Marowitz arrived in the UK in the summer of 1956. During 1963 and 1964 Charles Marowitz and Peter Brook put Artaud's theories into practice with the Royal Shakespeare Company Experimental Group/Theatre of Cruelty at LAMDA. This was the first full-fledged experimental project of its kind in Britain and injected Artaud's ideas into contemporaneous theatre practice. Marowitz directed the 1966 production of Joe Orton's *Loot* which received the Evening Standard Award for Best Play of the Year.

In 1968 Marowitz started the Open Space Theatre on Tottenham Court Road in collaboration with Thelma Holt (Marowitz 1990). The Open Space introduced many important American writers to the British Theatre including Sam Shepard, Mike Weller, and John Guare. The Open Space also included British writers such as Howard Barker. In many respects the Open Space was an Off Off Broadway Theatre based in London. It hosted an American season of plays in 1969 and continued to premiere many more American plays. The Open Space was known for environmental pieces, Shakespeare collages, and premieres of new writing, including the world premiere of *The Four Little Girls* by Pablo Picasso (Schiele 2005).

Chapter Six: Nancy Meckler

Nancy Meckler arrived in London in April 1968 after working at the La MaMa Plexus in New York. Nancy Meckler and her company, Freehold, were pioneers in using the body rather than words as the primary means of expression (Craig 1980: 106–107). Freehold would help to introduce 'physical theatre' to the British theatrical landscape. Meckler's style of theatre was based on the most vital concept evolved by the American avant-garde groups of the 1950s and 1960s: the body as a supersensitive instrument of expression. Meckler's style of theatre was a direct attack on the most ubiquitous stage convention in the western tradition—namely, drama as literature. For her and the company she created, the body had to bear the main burden of theatrical expression: the text was often viewed as a disguised tool of repression (Ansorge 1975: 26). Freehold's most successful work was an anti-war adaptation of *Antigone* (1969–70). It marked a shift away from purely literary reinterpretation and involved physical gymnastics and an orientation based on the impetus provided by the Peace Movement in America (Craig 1980: 106). Meckler was co-director of Shared Experience from 1987 until it disbanded in 2013. She continues to work regularly with the RSC.

Chapter Seven: Ed Berman

Ed Berman and his company Inter-Action were extremely influential in pioneering unconventional modes of community performance in unconventional locations for non-traditional theatre going audiences. Berman first came to England from Harvard University in 1962 as a Rhodes Scholar at Oxford. He began as a playwright and in 1968 started the first permanent lunchtime theatre in the UK. Over the next decade Inter-Action would be responsible for an extremely prolific range of community arts and professional theatre activities in dozens of venues. This included the activities of the British American Repertory Company. Berman's company had the express aim of interweaving community work with professional theatre activities. Inter-Action had a charitable framework and its workers engaged in a communal living arrangement (Itzin

1980: 51–59). During the 1970s extremely important experimental theatre groups such as the Women's Theatre Group, Monstrous Regiment, and Gay Sweatshop emerged out of, or were greatly influenced by, identity- and community-based seasons of plays produced by Ed Berman at the Almost Free Theatre.

Chapter Eight: Conclusion

American influence on the alternative theatre in Britain 1956–1980 was substantial and was also to an extent mutual. This chapter will draw conclusions and detail the underlying reasons why this phenomenon took place. It will also identify and detail the defining characteristics of American influence during this period, with respect to subject matter, performance efficacies, and cultural shifts. The book endeavours to demonstrate that there was a discernible pattern of American influence on the alternative theatre movement in Britain 1956 to 1980, which, while it has been recognised by others, has not been fully explored and analysed.

To summarise, this book describes a collection of American experimental theatre and performance practices which came to influence the practices of the alternative theatre movement in Britain. What happened in the post-war era was the evolution of a theatre diametrically opposed to the conventions of drama as literature common in the West since the Renaissance. It was an approach that rejected the beliefs and expectations of traditional audiences, complemented experimental influences developing in Europe like the work of Grotowski and Fo, and radically altered both the aesthetic and organisational basis upon which performance was created. These cultural and ideological intersections in turn helped to shape the ideological identity of the alternative theatre movement during this period.

Chapter Two: Background 1936–1956

The relationship between Britain and America is closer than ever. Since Churchill the relationship between the two countries has been described as a 'special relationship'. Cultural, political, and military links are expressed globally from Hollywood to Syria. Britain looks to America for trends and values and vice versa. The difficulty of translating plays is also rendered unnecessary because both nations are English speaking. America has also been a dominant force in world cinema since the end of World War I (Hollywood) which means that British children grow up learning a great deal about American culture and history. All of this is compounded by the British economic interdependence on the United States as demonstrated by the recent recession which started in America but soon had a knock-on effect in Britain. The recent economic recovery has also followed this pattern.

In his *Guardian* newspaper column, Michael Billington has raised the question of why, as he sees it, British theatres today have become so 'troublingly' dependent on American productions.

> I saw four American plays on successive nights last week—Tracy Letts's *August: Osage County*; Neil LaBute's *In A Dark Dark House*; Tarell Alvin McCraney's *Wig Out!*; and William Saroyan's *The Time of Your Life*. But, while I would count the Steppenwolf production of the Letts play among the great experiences of the year and enjoyed the Saroyan, such a transatlantic deluge left me thinking about the defining qualities of American drama and our unquestioning cultural enslavement to the United States. (Michael Billington, 'United Stages of America', *Guardian*, 3 December 2008)

In order to understand how the 'special relationship' as redefined by Michael Billington developed and in particular how changes in British culture relate to this book we will now examine the origins of American cultural and ideological transactions with British alternative theatre. As such the purpose of this chapter is to establish a background context and identify certain patterns which would later become characteristic of American influence on the alternative theatre movement in Britain 1956–1980. This book dates the beginning of American influence on the alternative theatre in Britain to the 1936 British premiere of *Waiting for Lefty* and the performance efficacy brought to bear through participatory performance practices. In order to understand how the 'troubling' relationship discussed by Michael Billington developed and in particular how changes in British culture relate to this study we will now examine the origins of American cultural and ideological transactions with British alternative theatre.

This chapter also seeks to demonstrate that theatre has often been used to define or challenge national values and the notion of the nation. Particularly at times of national crisis the theatre has served as a political and ideological tool to help reconfigure the nation. Rather than focusing on standard hegemonic forms of nationalism, this chapter will concentrate on counter-hegemonic discourses in Britain and America between 1936 and 1956. The chapter analyses groups that formulated a positive identity for marginalised or oppressed communities in Britain and America, and that posited an identity for the particular nation that privileged rather than minimised the position of these groups.

In this context influences such as that of American theatre and theatre practitioners on British theatre form part of a key cultural contestation of theatrical national identity and the theatre of particular communities within the nation. Likewise, certain groups will confront the homogenous image represented by the dominant group by asserting a more pluralistic or counter-hegemonic identity. The contribution of this book to this debate is in the way in which the impact of international influences is explored in the development of theatre within the context of a specific national theatrical culture.

In order to understand a phenomenon it is necessary to examine its roots. As in other countries, the concept of the nation in America has responded to social change and times of crisis. Theatre and other media have contributed to the changing discourse about national values and national identity (Mason and Gainor, eds. 1999: 9). Unlike the nations of Europe that could claim the organic development of a national spirit through a common history, folklore, literature, ethnicity, and language, America's common identity needed to be more artificially constructed because of its diversity of ethnicities, religions, languages, and customs. Despite severe social prejudice, a hierarchical social structure, and legalised forms of social discrimination, some of the factors that were represented as uniting the country were the English language, Anglo-Saxon Protestant culture, and a common dream of prosperity founded on notions of liberty, equality, and free enterprise.

The image of America as a land of opportunity for the hardworking individual applied to immigrants and citizens alike and fostered the concept of a national community of individuals who could all prosper. Despite widespread anti-Catholicism, Jim Crow laws, the confinement to reservations of Native Americans, the Chinese Exclusion Act, and other forms of ethnic and religious discrimination, the image of a national homogenous population of white Protestants persisted and was reinforced by the metaphor of a national melting pot in which all the diverse elements could end up emulating the white Protestant archetype (Meserve 1965: 73). Despite cultural pressures toward homogeneity, American theatre has seen various marginalised and excluded groups (Women, African Americans, Latinos, Asian Americans, Native Americans, Gays, and Lesbians) use theatre to reverse the stereotypical images conveyed by the mainstream theatre and other media.

Historically speaking the Armoury Show of 1913 which toured New York, Chicago, and Boston was the first major exhibition of 'modern art' in the United States and served as a starting point for the development of distinctive American artwork. In the United States during the 1920s and 1930s the avant-garde in art was associated with Left-wing political movements and the work produced was generally politically engaged and highly accessible. Black Mountain College in North Carolina was established in 1933 as an experimental institution which brought together members of the Bauhaus and European artists fleeing the Nazis. Bauhaus teachers had included some of the most important artists of the modernist era including Wassily Kandinsky, Paul Klee, and Joseph Albers. After its closure in 1933 Albers and his wife Anni set up Black Mountain College which was a tremendous incubator for the American avant-garde and helped to launch the careers of such figures as Eric Bentley, William and Elaine de Kooning, Robert Rauschenberg, Merce Cunningham, Arthur Penn, and John Cage. Many artists taught at Black Mountain College during the summer in exchange for room and board and the opportunity to experiment.

Perhaps the best known work produced in the twenty-four-year existence of Black Mountain College was John Cage's *Theater Piece No. 1* which is regarded as the first 'Happening'. Cage first arrived at Black Mountain College in 1948 as Merce Cunningham's accompanist. In 1952 Cage performed his 4'33", in which a pianist sits in silence at a piano for exactly four minutes and thirty-three seconds. Inspired by his ideas about Zen, music composition, and duration rather than conventional harmony as well as Antonin Artaud's ideas about integrating theatre with its audience, Cage then conceived of *Theater Piece No. 1*. He collaborated with Cunningham, Robert Rauschenberg, M.C. Richards, and Charles Olson on the diverse elements of the piece which were then organised into a compartmented structure. Back in New York, Cage and Rauschenberg continued to collaborate on performances with Merce Cunningham's dance company. Their work then influenced the artist Allan Kaprow who coined the term 'Happening' in 1959 when he staged *18 Happenings in 6 Parts* at the Reuben Gallery in New York. Kaprow would later help to introduce 'Happenings' to the UK and this will be discussed further in Chapter Four.

As mentioned in the introductory chapter, following the American entry into World War II three million Americans passed through Great Britain between 1942 and 1945. It was the largest ever encounter between Americans and the British people in history. At one point before the D-Day invasion Americans made up six percent of the resident population of Great Britain (Reynolds 1995: 431–433). By the end of World War II the joint Gross Domestic Product of Europe had fallen by about twenty-five percent, while the Gross National Product of the United States had risen during the war years by over fifty percent in real terms (Clarke 2008: xiv). Britain was saddled with enormous war debt while America avoided any damage to its mainland. Britain survived the war but the cost would ultimately lead to the loss of empire (Clarke 2008: 508–512). Britain's war debts were not fully repaid to the United States and Canada until the year 2006. The Cold War solidified the current arrangement of US military bases scattered throughout the UK.

As has already been noted, as late as the 1920s Britain controlled a quarter of the world's territory and a quarter of its total population. However, primarily as a consequence of changes necessitated by or arising from World War II, the British Empire was to a large extent dismantled. During the post-war period there was also a shift of power and influence both in politics and culture to the United States. These changes can be formally dated from the Quebec conference in September 1944 which involved Churchill, Roosevelt, and other war time allies as they began to plan for a post-war scenario. For the British this would ultimately involve the loss of India and Palestine. The Commonwealth as it exists today was formulated in 1949 as a free association of equal and independent countries, in effect to replace the Empire, though the process of decolonisation took two more decades to be fulfilled (Clarke 2008: 505).

There is general agreement that the American Theatre really came of age only after World War I. At that time a group of serious and exciting new writers emerged who won the respect of critics and audiences alike. Among these writers were Maxwell Anderson, Elmer Rice, and most notably Eugene O'Neill who introduced the naturalism and symbolism of Ibsen, Strindberg, and Chekhov to the American theatre. Works such as *Anna Christie* (1921) by Eugene O'Neill and *Street Scene* (1929) by Elmer Rice generated an interest in American theatre abroad. There were also notable commercial works by American composers such as George Gershwin, Cole Porter, and Richard Rogers.

In the first decade following World War II American theatrical practice began to have a considerable impact on British theatre. In his book *Mid-Century Drama* (1962) the British theatre historian Laurence Kitchen described American theatre as the most powerful foreign influence on the London stage during the ten years following the end of the war. The American influence he describes is outlined in a chapter called *The Potent Intruder* which begins with a review of Marowitz's 1958 production of Odets' *Waiting for Lefty* in the upstairs theatre at the British Drama League. American dramatists known prior to World War II whose works continued to be performed in London after the war included Lillian Hellman, Clifford Odets, Eugene O'Neill, Thornton Wilder, Maxwell Anderson, Philip Barry, Sidney Kingsley, and William Saroyan. Several commercial writers of comedies and lighter entertainments belonging to the same generation also had plays presented in the West End in the post-war period.

In 1948 a new generation of 'serious' American drama started to flow into Britain with the London premiere of Arthur Miller's *All My Sons*. *Death of a Salesman* and Tennessee Williams's *The Glass Menagerie* came in 1949 along with the British premiere of Williams's *A Streetcar Named Desire*. These productions will be discussed in greater detail later on in this chapter. British theatre was influenced, beside the newer playwrights, by other works by members of the pre-World War II generation of American playwrights produced in London including revivals: in 1952 *Montserrat* Hellman's rendering of the French play opened at the Lyric Theatre in Hammersmith and ran for thirty-nine performances but did not transfer to the West End. Lillian Hellman's *The Children's Hour* was revived at the Arts Theatre in 1956. Maxwell Anderson's dramatic adaptation of *The Bad Seed* in 1955 had a run of 196 performances. In 1954 *The Matchmaker* by Thornton Wilder opened at the Haymarket Theatre and ran for 275 performances. Ten years later it was transformed into a musical *Hello Dolly* which was a tremendous commercial hit. Popular playwrights who belonged to an older generation had some spectacular successes as well as disastrous failures. Paul Osborne's original play *Mornings at Seven* was first staged in New York in 1939 and had its London premiere in 1953 and ran for forty-six performances and received a lukewarm critical response.

Additional American playwrights who became well known during the 1950s and had works produced in Britain included Robert Anderson, William Gibson, Paddy Chayefsky, Frank Gilroy, and Gore Vidal. Jean Kerr, Ira Levin, Liam O'Brien, John Patrick, Neil Simon, Samuel Taylor, and the team of Joseph Fields and Peter DeVries all had commercial successes. John Patrick's *The Teahouse of the August Moon* ranked first in the number of performances within this group. The play opened at Her Majesty's Theatre on

April 22, 1954 and closed on August 11, 1956 after 954 performances.

Throughout the 1950s, then, the flow of American works to London continued to expand in the number and variety of productions and Miller and Williams wrote plays that made them the leading American playwrights of their generation. It was against this background and in this context that the next stage of American influence, the import of American experimental theatre and performance practices, developed. That stage, which is the focus of this book, coalesced with the cultural revolution of the 1960s and contributed to an important new phase in the history of the alternative theatre movement in Britain.

The success of John Osborne's *Look Back in Anger* in 1956 has been seen by many as the crucial event that determined the re-orientation of British theatre in the late fifties, but there were other less visible milestones on the journey from stilted drawing-room drama to more diverse theatrical genres. The opening up of the London stage after the war to creative contact with New York and Paris, for example, was an event every bit as important for the evolution of twentieth-century English drama as the advent of Osborne, Wesker and the other 'new wave' dramatists (Shellard, 1999:17).

The American influence on British cultural institutions was also substantial and long-lasting. The potential foundation for the non-commercial sector of theatre in Britain was laid by three organisations: E.N.S.A. (Entertainment National Service Association); the civilian Drama Section of C.E.M.A. (Council for the Encouragement of Music and the Arts); and the Play Unit of A.B.C.A. (Army Bureau of Current Affairs). The founding of the Council for the Encouragement of Music and the Arts (C.E.M.A.) in January 1940 led to the formation of the Arts Council of Great Britain in August 1946 and therefore the non-commercial sector of British theatre. The Play Unit of the Army Bureau of Current Affairs was run by people who were primarily from the London Unity Theatre which began by performing American plays from the Group Theatre in New York. The Entertainment National Service Association was started in 1938 by Basil Dean.

The Council for the Encouragement of Music and the Arts was established in 1940 with the financial support of an American-funded organisation called the Pilgrim Trust. C.E.M.A.'s purpose was to help support cultural activity and boost public morale in Britain during wartime. Before this there was no sustained public subsidy of theatre in Britain. On the other hand theatre was taxed, dating back to 1916, and the price of submitting a play to the office of the Lord Chamberlain was two shillings, whether or not it was successful in receiving a license. As Kenneth Tynan put it of this period,

> The truth is that governments have two equally effective means of controlling these artists. One is by direct censorship. The other is more oblique but no less potent—it is censorship imposed by withholding subsidies, thereby enslaving the artist to the box-office and forcing him, unless he is a genius, to turn out lovable, undisturbing after-dinner entertainments. (Tynan 1975: 355)

Having outlined this general context, this chapter will now examine and trace individual elements of American influence on theatrical practices in Britain before and after World War II.

Unity Theatre

The story of Unity Theatre is of critical importance in understanding the history of the alternative theatre movement in Britain. It is a story of British innovation based to some extent on a trans-Atlantic transmission of theatrical practices to British theatre during the 1930's. The first plays produced by Unity Theatre were originally from the Group Theatre in New York. Much like the Unity

Theatre phenomenon in Scotland and England, Left-leaning theatres in the United States such as the Group Theatre (1931–1941) were a part of a national infrastructure for performing plays around the country with the intention of increasing class solidarity and participation in a popular front. These theatres were created for the explicit purpose of changing society through performance.

In 1935 the Roosevelt government initiated the Federal Theatre Project, which absorbed some of the radicalism of this movement, and at the same time contained it within a government funded institution. Many of the plays as well as innovative practices which the Unity Theatre later produced and adopted were first developed by the Group Theatre or with the support of the Federal Theatre Project in the United States (Chambers, 1989: 77). The Group Theatre was dedicated to eliminating what it perceived as the artificiality of contemporaneous Broadway productions, and to influencing social issues of the day through theatre. In the economic climate of the 1930s meanwhile the number of unemployed people in the United States increased dramatically and those who made their living from the theatre were no less affected by the Great Depression. Just like other skilled but unemployed workers theatre professionals were eligible for help from volunteer organisations as well as state and federal relief programs. On April 8, 1935 the United States Congress created the Works Progress Administration designed to foster a new approach to the problem of mass unemployment. Under the guidelines of the W.P.A. healthy and able bodied persons were to be taken off of the relief programmes of individual states and offered work within their own skills and trades.

The W.P.A. insisted that workers in the arts including painters, musicians, writers, and actors were as deserving of federal support as workers with other skills and during a National Theatre Conference at the University of Iowa in the summer of 1935 the W.P.A. announced the creation of a 'free, adult, uncensored' federal theatre (O'Connor and Brown 1980: 10). The Federal Theatre Project emerged as part of a division of the W.P.A. along with the Federal Music Project, Federal Art Project, and Federal Writers Project. Together these groups combined to employ over 40,000 artists by the end of 1935. The Federal Theatre Project existed from 1935 to 1939 and was most active in New York although it had units in forty states.

The American contribution to Unity Theatre, however, consisted primarily in providing a repertoire of material to get started with, although the interest continued, and also the important influence of the Living Newspaper which in the United States grew out of the Federal Theatre Project. The Federal Theatre Project is perhaps best remembered for the Living Newspaper the most popular of which were, *Triple-A Ploughed Under* (1936) about the government's farm subsidy programme, *Power* (1937) about rural electrification and flood control, and *One Third of a Nation* (1938) about slum housing. In 1943 Unity revived the Living Newspaper *One Third of a Nation* in London (Chambers 1989: 405). The title comes from Franklin D. Roosevelt's second inaugural address referring to those Americans who were ill-housed, ill-clad, and ill-nourished.

The Living Newspaper was a new dramatic form influenced by agitprop and was intended as a kind of documentary that informed its audience of the nature and origin of social problems and then called upon its audience to take specific action. The Living Newspaper brought together unemployed newspaper workers and theatre artists. Originally the Living Newspaper unit in New York attempted to produce a Living Newspaper about the Ethiopian war in 1936 but the White House directly intervened and cancelled the production (O'Connor and Brown 1980: 10). The reason it was cancelled was the Roosevelt administration thought that the Living Newspaper could potentially antagonise the government of Fascist

Italy. This cancellation clearly highlights the potential efficacy of this form of performance practice.

Then there was a successful Living Newspaper called *Triple-A Ploughed Under* which reported on recent events which had affected farmers as well as food prices with reference to a recent milk strike in 1932. The production incorporated projections, music, masks, spotlights, loudspeakers, and actors planted in the audience all of which was intended to shock the audience into organised social action. The New York production was directed by Joseph Losey and H. Gordon Graham and ran for eighty-five performances before being subsequently produced again in Chicago, Cleveland, Los Angeles, and Milwaukee. Unity Theatre in Britain forged direct links with Living Newspaper originators in America and then produced several indigenous British Living Newspapers. Arthur Arent the original author of *Triple A Plowed Under* visited Unity and shared his experiences and Andre van Gyseghem an important Unity director who worked with Paul Robeson in Britain and also visited America to observe Living Newspapers.

Living Newspaper performances in Britain and America introduced topical subject matter and helped to form class consciousness. The performances changed the relations of individual audience members to the dramatic performance. There was an ideological transaction brought to bear through both form and content. Although theatrical developments in the period 1936–1956 occurred before the main focus of this book, innovations during the period nonetheless marks the origin of American influence on alternative theatre in Britain from 1956–1980 and set in motion certain patterns in terms of performance practices, repertoire, and public subsidy which would influence later developments, which will be detailed further in the following chapters.

In the autumn of 1934 members of the New Theatre League, meantime, which was a confederation of Left-leaning political theatre groups, visited a meeting of the Group Theatre's communist cell and asked them to contribute a short play for one of their regularly scheduled Sunday theatrical events. Among the members of the communist cell were Elia Kazan and Clifford Odets and the members of the cell agreed to collaborate on a play about a strike with each actor responsible for writing one scene of the play. However as the January deadline for the performance piece neared none of the actors in the group had taken the time to write their individual scene. Because of this Clifford Odets isolated himself for three nights and wrote *Waiting for Lefty* (Clurman 1983: 141).

Waiting for Lefty was first performed on 6 January 1935 as part of the New Theatre League's theatrical bill at the Civic Repertory Theatre on Fourteenth Street in New York City and later transferred to Broadway. At the end of the play the audience rises to their feet with the actors and joins them on stage in calling for a strike. It was an electrifying and ground breaking moment in the history of participatory performance practice which would become an important characteristic of the alternative theatre movement. Performance efficacy is generated in such a context because performance practices have the potential to change the direction of a given community.

The first formal production at Unity was a double bill which opened on 17 April 1936 at the Britannia Street Theatre in London. The plays were *Waiting for Lefty* written in 1935 by Clifford Odets and *Private Hicks* also written in 1935 by Albert Maltz. *Waiting for Lefty* became emblematic of Unity itself and Unity staged the play over 300 times for more than 40,000 people (Chambers 1989: 65) even before the outbreak of World War II. The potential for performance efficacy was elevated from the micro level of an individual performance to a macro level of potential influence on British society and culture. Another early success for Unity was the British premiere of *Bury the Dead* (1936) by Irwin Shaw about common soldiers who are often forced to fight in conflicts which are not their own.

The members of Unity obtained their scripts for these plays primarily from an American magazine called *New Theater*. In the first instance American playwrights were used as opposed to those from Germany or the Soviet Union because of a common language. In fact the members of the American Group Theatre who in 1937 were in London for a West End production of Odets's *Golden Boy* met and interacted with the Unity Theatre. They attended both the opening night and a subsequent performance of *Plant in the Sun* by Group Theatre writer Ben Bengal with Paul Robeson in the lead role. Members of Unity met with Elia Kazan, Harold Clurman, Lee J. Cobb, Stella Adler, and Odets himself who spoke from the Unity stage (Chambers 1989: 158). The introduction of American methods derived from Stanislavski would in time change British Theatre, particularly with regard to attitudes towards improvisation. The members of the Group Theatre suggested that Unity should establish a professional wing which they did within six months and the Group Theatre members also attended a meeting in the House of Commons along with Robeson in 1938 in support of an appeal for funds by a group of MPs on behalf of Unity.

An equally proud moment came when members of the internationally famous American Group Theatre—the main inspiration for many in the British left-wing theatre movement—congratulated Unity on its production of *Plant in the Sun* and returned to see it twice. The Group Theatre represented the best of American drama, and with writers such as Clifford Odets, Irwin Shaw, Albert Maltz, and Ben Bengal, had been the main source of Unity's repertoire (Chambers 1989: 158).

Paul Robeson (1898–1976)

Paul Robeson was an African-American singer, actor, athlete, and civil rights activist. He was born in Princeton, New Jersey on April 9, 1898. His father was a runaway slave. At the age of seventeen Robeson won an academic scholarship to Rutgers University where he was twice named as an All-American football player. He graduated as Valedictorian of his class and then went on to law school at Columbia University in New York. After receiving his law degree he took a job in a law firm but left after a white secretary refused to take dictation from him. He then devoted himself to his artistic talents in music and theatre and the promotion of civil rights. In London, Robeson earned acclaim at the Savoy Theatre in 1930 as only the second black actor in history to play the role of Othello. The African-American actor Ira Aldridge is considered to be the first black actor to play the role of Othello in 1833. In London Robeson also performed in Eugene O'Neill's *Emperor Jones* and *All God's Chillun Got Wings* but is best remembered for his singing in *Showboat* (1927).

Robeson who sang at the opening of Unity Theatre later returned in 1937 to play the lead role in a production of *Planet in the Sun* by Ben Bengal. The play is about a group of workers who organise a strike at a candy factory in New York following the management's ruthless tactics to prevent them from unionising. In order to participate in the Unity production Robeson was willing to perform anonymously and for free and also turned down the starring role in a production of *The Sun Never Sets* at the Drury Lane Theatre in London's West End (Chambers 1989: 152). The production of *Plant in the Sun* was reviewed by over twenty publications in Britain and the opening night performance was attended by a group of MPs as well as the future first prime minister of India Nehru who was a personal friend of Robeson's. In this context the potential for performance efficacy to directly shape attitudes within the British political establishment, and thereby British society and culture, was acute. Following the opening night 400 new members joined Unity and in 1939 the production won a national competition sponsored by the British Drama League which was judged and announced by Tyrone Guthrie. Robeson would continue to serve as a member of the Unity Theatre general council (Chambers 1989: 151–159).

Clifford Odets (1906–1963)

Clifford Odets was born to Jewish immigrant parents in Philadelphia, Pennsylvania on 18 July 1906. He was raised in New York City and dropped out of school at the age of seventeen to become an actor. He became an original member of the New York based Left-wing Group Theatre founded by Harold Clurman, Cheryl Crawford, and Lee Strasberg. Odets wrote his first produced play for the Group Theatre in 1934 inspired by a taxi driver strike of the same year. *Waiting for Lefty* was originally produced in 1935 and was followed by *Awake and Sing* (1935), and *Till the Day I Die* (1935), which were also produced on Broadway. Odets's *Golden Boy* was produced in 1937 and was the Group Theatre's biggest commercial success. Odets would also write *Rocket to the Moon* (1938), *Night Music* (1940), and the Group Theatre's last production *Clash by Night* (1941). He also wrote *The Big Knife* (1949) and *The Country Girl* (1950).

The London Unity Theatre would produce a number of his plays including *Waiting for Lefty* (which was awarded second place in a national competition hosted by the British Drama League in 1940), *I Can't Sleep, Till the Day I Die, Awake and Sing,* and *Golden Boy*. The Glasgow Unity Theatre which was formed in 1941 produced Odets' *Awake and Sing* as their opening production and two more of Odets' plays including *Golden Boy* and *Till the Day I Die* (Chambers 1989: 245). Although not Unity productions Odets'

Awake in Sing was revived in 1950 and he had a substantial commercial hit in *Winter Journey* during 1952. Additionally, there was a modest run of the *Big Knife* in 1954.

Eugene O'Neill (1888–1953)

Among the writers who were well-established prior to World War II Eugene O'Neill consistently received the greatest praise in the post-war period. His later works attracted close attention. Two of these including *Iceman Cometh* and *A Long Day's Journey into Night* which both led British critics to generally agree that in these works O'Neill surpassed his previous achievements. At the Arts Theatre Club *The Iceman Cometh* had its London debut in January 1958 and received rave reviews. A month later it transferred to the Winter Garden which was a much larger commercial theatre and played for thirty-one additional performances.

O'Neill's posthumous work *A Long Day's Journey into Night* first appeared in Stockholm on February 10, 1956.There was a New York production in the autumn of 1956 which starred Fredric March and Jason Robards Jr. In New York it ran for 389 performances. In 1958 the British premiere of *A Long Day's Journey into Night* opened with a British cast including Anthony Quayle, Gwen Davies, and Alan Bates at the Royal Lyceum Theatre in Edinburgh. Later that year it transferred to the Globe Theatre in London and ran for 108 performances. O'Neill posthumously received his fourth Pulitzer Prize for the play and many critics at the time considered it to be O'Neill's masterpiece.

O'Neill's trilogy *Mourning Becomes Electra* had its original London production in 1938 and for the following two decades *Mourning Becomes Electra* continued to interest companies and critics in the UK as it was the work which may have triggered O'Neill's being awarded the Nobel Prize in Literature in 1936. The Arts Theatre revived *Mourning Becomes Electra* in 1955 and it ran for two months. In 1961 the Old Vic presented twenty-four performances of the play in repertory and there was another revival in 1967 at the Traverse Theatre in Edinburgh.

Tennessee Williams (1911–1983)

Like Arthur Miller, Tennessee Williams had his first two commercially successful plays produced in London at the end of the 1940s. *The Glass Menagerie* starring Helen Hayes in her London debut opened at the Haymarket Theatre on July 28, 1948. *A Streetcar Named Desire* with Vivien Leigh as Blanche DuBois and directed by her husband Sir Laurence Olivier opened at the Aldwych Theatre in late 1949. In the first instance these American works in Britain were highly provocative and it is worthwhile to examine their reception at the time. Both Helen Hayes and Vivien Leigh won rave reviews for their acting but the plays themselves were both harshly attacked. *The Glass Menagerie* closed after a modest run and initially failed to attract a large audience.

A Streetcar Named Desire managed to overcome the sensational advanced notoriety and an outpouring of disgust and widespread indignation upon its West End opening and achieved a commercially successful run. Generally, however, the influential critics thought the production was unworthy of its star and director. There was even an effort to have the play withdrawn because of elements considered obscene. While the first London production of *A Streetcar Named Desire* had a commercially viable run and acquainted the British public with Tennessee Williams's most famous work it did not do much at the time to enhance his reputation with British theatre critics who generally failed to recognise Williams as a playwright of the first order.

The production also led to a subsequent controversy involving Parliament because the Arts Council had decided to grant the production tax exemption on the grounds that it was partly cultural and partly educational. Tennent Productions which in many ways embodied establishment commercial theatre changed itself into a non-profit registered charity in order to avoid paying the Entertainment Tax which amounted to 10% of gross profits and accounted for over a quarter of the price of a ticket (Shellard 1999: 25).

It had become a normal practice for theatrical managements to take advantage of legislation which was originally intended to encourage more theatre productions during the First World War. However in this specific instance Tennent Productions was challenged by Members of Parliament. There was then an investigation by a Select Committee in the House of Commons into the practice of theatrical managements forming non-profit subsidiaries in conjunction with the practice of the Arts Council forming simultaneous associations with the commercial managements in order to permit them to avoid the Entertainment Tax. This investigation was in reaction to the West End production of *A Streetcar Named Desire* (Shellard 2005: 26). The investigation generated a substantial financial setback for Tennent Productions which became liable for hitherto unpaid income taxes dating back to 1945.

While plays by Tennessee Williams did not originally win full approval from the majority of British theatre critics it is also important to recognise that his works were not roundly denounced either. Initially they failed to attract large audiences and complete long commercially successful runs in mainstream West End theatres. However, over time the reception to his work developed to the point where his plays are now consistently revived throughout Britain on a regular basis. These include *Summer and Smoke* (1951), *Camino Real* (1957), and *The Rose Tattoo* (1959). In addition to these commercial productions, there were also non-commercial productions of four plays including *Garden District* produced at the Arts Theatre Club in 1955 which ran for five weeks and *Orpheus Descending* which was performed at the Royal Court in 1959.

Arthur Miller (1915–2005)

Arthur Miller achieved some early success with critics and theatregoers in Britain that nearly matched his recognition in the United States. *All My Sons* and *Death of a Salesman* were Miller's first successes in New York and were subsequently produced in London in 1948 and 1949. The productions received mixed reviews and *All My Sons* was not a commercial success although *Death of a Salesman* enjoyed a relatively successful run from the point of view of ticket sales. In 1956 Arthur Miller's *The Crucible* and *A View from the Bridge* re-opened in London and both plays made an impact on the British theatrical landscape.

The Crucible first generated excitement in British theatre circles in 1954 when it was presented by the Bristol Old Vic Company at the Theatre Royal Bristol. The leading British theatre critics, representing the large daily newspapers and weekly periodicals, reviewed the production and in general found it to be an important and provocative work. In London *The Crucible* opened on April 9, 1956 at the Royal Court and was presented by the English Stage Company during its historic first season. The following month this newly formed theatre group premiered John Osborne's *Look Back in Anger* on May 8, 1956. While Miller's play was well received critically it was intended as only one of a series of plays and as a consequence ran for only thirty-six performances.

I turn now to cultural change as evidenced by alterations in censorship, alterations brought about by the performance of American plays dealing with 'forbidden' topics. As this chapter considers the period 1936–1956 this preliminary phase of American influence on alternative theatre in Britain can be seen as culminating in 1956 with the New Watergate Theatre Club season of American plays at the Comedy Theatre. At the time it was unique for a club to produce a season of plays in a large West End theatre, particularly plays that all deal with homosexuality. Homosexuality was a criminal offence in Britain at the time and remained so until 1967.

New Watergate Theatre Club at the Comedy Theatre

During the 1950s American plays like *A View from the Bridge* (1955/6), *Cat on a Hot Tin Roof* (1955), and *Tea & Sympathy* (1953) challenged the system of theatre censorship in Britain. In 1956 the New Watergate Theatre Club produced a season involving these American plays at the Comedy Theatre in London's West End. All three dealt with the theme of homosexuality or what the Lord Chamberlain's readers previously referred to as 'the forbidden subject' (Tynan 2007: 38). Small theatres in Britain such as Unity and the New Watergate became clubs in order to circumvent the censor. As I have noted already, unlike plays written in the UK, these American plays were not created with the British licensing provision in mind. They were, moreover, written by highly visible award-winning Broadway playwrights and as such generated interest from producers, critics, and the theatre-going public in Britain.

The season originally came about because Robert Anderson sent the eventual producer Anthony Field a copy of his play *Tea and Sympathy*. Field was interested in producing the play in London but it had to get passed by the Lord Chamberlain. The response from the Lord Chamberlain was, 'No, the whole basis of the play of *Tea and Sympathy* is not acceptable and you can't do it in a public theatre' (Anthony Field, http://sounds.bl.uk: Theatre Archive Project: 2007: 2). Field was also interested in producing Tennessee Williams's play *Cat on a Hot Tin Roof* but again the Lord Chamberlain banned the play from public performance. Arthur Miller had also sent Field *A View From the Bridge* which again the Lord Chamberlain rejected.

Field knew a lady named Muriel Large who ran the Watergate Theatre Club, a small theatre club under the arches at Charing Cross Station. In London at that time there were between twenty and thirty small theatre clubs and they could do plays that did not have to be passed by the Lord Chamberlain. Large was looking for plays to produce and Field suggested the idea of doing the three American plays although they had large casts for a small club theatre and they would be expensive because of the American royalties. After reading the plays Large suggested transferring the Watergate Club into the Comedy Theatre although no one had ever run an 850-seat West End theatre as a club. They discussed the idea with a number of people including Hugh (Binkie) Beaumont, as well as Field's boss at the time Harold Wingate. Binkie Beaumont was a ubiquitous West End manager and producer who ran the company H.M. Tennent and Harold Wingate was a West End producer who was responsible for the Comedy Theatre. They then decided to take a chance and branded the enterprise the New Watergate Theatre Club at the Comedy Theatre.

During the season Tennent and Wingate had to be very strict and people had to first buy a membership for a pound. People could then buy tickets after they had been a member of the club for twenty-four hours and bring up to three guests. The police were very vigilant and ensured that the box office was complying with the club membership laws. If the box office had not, the club would have been shut down immediately.

A View from the Bridge opened at the Comedy Theatre and was directed by Peter Brook. Miller actually rewrote the play for the London production changing the original one-act version previously staged in New York in 1955 into a full-length work. The British critics complained about aspects that struck them as sensational and sentimental. However, the production had a successful run of 220 performances. The main character Eddie Carbone harbours taboo incestuous feelings towards his wife's orphaned niece Catherine whom they have raised. It is also revealed that Eddie and his wife Beatrice have not slept together for several months. When his wife's cousins Rodolpho and Marco arrive from Italy illegally the attraction between Rodolpho and Catherine is perceived by Eddie as a threat. Rodolpho is blonde and sings opera and Eddie projects his homophobia onto him and tries to portray him as effeminate and sexually abnormal. When Eddie, in a rage, finds a post-coital Rodolpho and Catherine he grabs his niece and kisses her on the mouth. Rodolpho says that he wants to marry Catherine and Eddie, 'pins his arms, laughing, and suddenly kisses him' (*A View From the Bridge*, Miller 1956: 63). The moment is full of dramatic tension and it is this male kiss that would mean the play would be censored in Britain if it had not been performed under club conditions.

Cat on a Hot Tin Roof was a critical and commercial success in New York and received the Pulitzer Prize for Drama in 1955. The play opened in London in 1956 and was directed by Peter Hall. Kim Stanley, an American star, played the role of Maggie but the play achieved only a moderately successful run of 132 performances. It is a play about 'Mendacity' people's self-deception as well as their everyday lying to other people. The character of Brick is in a state of spiritual disrepair precipitated by the apparent suicide of his close friend Skipper. In the second act, which is devoted primarily to Brick and Big Daddy, Brick finally tells his father that he is dying and Big Daddy forces Brick to acknowledge Skipper confessed his love in a phone conversation and Brick then hung up the phone. However it is interesting just how little is actually said regarding the topic of homosexuality. Skipper is a spectre present through his very absence and haunts Brick and Maggie's lives and the action of the play but the topic of homosexuality was so provocative in British theatre at the time that the play could only be performed under club conditions although any reference to homosexuality is heavily veiled and is barely referred to.

Tea and Sympathy by Robert Anderson also made an impact as part of the 1956 season at the Comedy Theatre. The recurrent subject matter throughout Anderson's writing and one which links him with the work of William Inge was the topic of sexuality and marriage. Although Anderson at times used nonrepresentational techniques his usual form has been described as falling within the parameters of the well-made play. He is primarily remembered as a writer for Broadway where six of his plays were produced although two of his film scripts also received Academy Award nominations. *Tea and Sympathy* was Anderson's first Broadway play and originally opened on 30 September 1953 and ran for 712 performances. The production was widely celebrated for Elia Kazan's direction and performances by Deborah Kerr (later Ingrid Bergman) and John Kerr. In *Tea and Sympathy* an older married woman offers herself to an adolescent boy after he has been falsely accused of homosexuality and needs to be reassured in his accepted masculine gender role. However, it is actually the antagonist in the play who projects his guilty feelings over his own latent homosexuality on to the boy.

The New Watergate Theatre Club season attracted an enormous amount of media attention primarily because Arthur Miller came to London with Marilyn Monroe whom he had married earlier that year. The three plays each ran eight or nine months which was remarkable for a club theatre in the West End. The major papers including *The Sunday Times* and *The Observer* acknowledged that these three plays were very important ones (Anthony Field, http://sounds.bl.uk: Theatre Archive Project: 2007: 2–4). The New

Watergate Theatre Club season also persuaded the Lord Chamberlain to drop opposition to the staging of plays about homosexuality (Chambers and Prior: 1987: 115). Opening this forbidden subject matter to theatrical experience and thus public discussion, at the individual and the social levels, did change British theatre practice and to some extent British society. These three plays would not have been censored because of their plots, but specifically because of their homosexual content and the New Watergate Theatre Club season is a great example of efficacy and social, cultural and political impact.

Conclusion

British productions of American plays pushed the boundaries of acceptable subject matter and would lay the groundwork for future American influence on experimental theatre and performance practices which will be discussed in forthcoming chapters. Further, as this chapter has shown, there was a direct exchange of American performance practices and forms such as the Living Newspaper to Britain during this period. The interrelationship of space, stage, audience, actor, and author affect the social and cultural efficacy of a given performance. With regard to this process, the democratising performance practices which were an inherent part of the Living Newspaper form and productions such as *Waiting for Lefty* empowered audiences in Britain and brought to bear new relationships with contemporaneous events challenging political, cultural, and social attitudes. This along with theatrical representations of hitherto underrepresented communities in Britain challenged the status quo.

In summary the number and variety of American theatrical works produced in London from 1936 to 1956, including those by commercial and subsidised theatres, indicates an abiding interest in American theatre. Critics and audiences often shared this interest. Analysing the fortunes of these American works in Britain offers a perspective from which to view American theatrical achievement and its influence on the British theatrical landscape during this period. Participatory performance practices would become a core characteristic of the Alternative Theatre movement in Britain. The trajectory of American influence on this performance practice in Britain can be traced to the inaugural April 1936 production of *Waiting for Lefty* at the London Unity Theatre.

We turn now to the theatre and performance practices of American alternative theatre groups during the 1950s and 1960s which were not based in Britain but did influence British alternative theatre.

Chapter Three: American Groups

During the 1950s, the white heterosexual male American exemplar was the dominant representation of American national identity in the media. The Hollywood Western was a ubiquitous movie genre in which white settlers would easily defeat 'savage' Indians played by Sicilian actors with blue eyes. General Eisenhower was elected as President of the United States in 1952, and former soldiers now in their thirties, channeled their energies into building American economic power. Against this backdrop counter-hegemonic voices emerged in the American theatre such as that of Edward Albee.

For example in his play, *The American Dream* (1961) the character of the young man describes himself as a 'clean cut, Midwest farm boy type' (Albee 1961: 31) and is recognised by the grandmother as 'the American dream', but he has lost any sense of feeling or compassion and will do anything for money. And in Britain Albee's *The American Dream* was produced at London's Royal Court Theatre in 1961, directed by Peter Yates. Indeed from the late 1950s onward, marginalised groups challenged the dominant social discourse through the Civil Rights movement, student protests, later demonstrations against the Vietnam War, and the widespread rejection of dominant cultural values.

During the period 1956 to 1980 the group, as opposed to the individual, became the focus of organisations associated with what came to be known as alternative society. This trend was reflected in the structure of alternative theatre organisations that emerged during this period. It was demonstrated in both their working processes and in the performance pieces they produced. The idea of a collective creation free of conventional and traditional hierarchical structures became the basis for a new method of conceiving and developing theatre and performance.

To a certain degree this was a reaction to what was perceived as fragmentation within established society and established theatre, fragmentation perceived to be based on competition and arbitrary concerns such as success and careerism (Shank 1972: 3). The focus on group living and group activity, in theatre and social arrangements, was based on the value of co-operation and an attempt to establish a sense of wholeness through collective creation. The most important pioneering groups were the Living Theatre (1946), Cafe La MaMa (1961), the Open Theatre (1963), Bread and Puppet Theatre (1963/64), Richard Schechner's Performance Group (1968), The Manhattan Project (1970), The Play-House of the Ridiculous (1965), and the San Francisco Mime Troupe (1959).

Characteristically members of alternative theatre groups were not exclusively performers but people with a broad range of creative responsibilities who made little distinction between working as a performer, director, designer, or playwright. Members applied their creative energies collectively in making a performance piece. While some provided more leadership than others, this work and experimentation was intended to produce collective expression and not the work of a fragmentary hierarchical process with individual artists working in isolation.

This chapter will detail and explore the impact on British theatre of the American-based alternative theatre groups which toured Britain during the period 1956–1980. It begins with a general overview of the area, then microscopes down into detailed description and analysis of the Living Theatre, Open Theatre, La MaMa, and Bread and Puppet respectively and their work and reception in Britain.

During the 1950s American plays played in London whereas during the 1960's US and British theatrical enterprise cohabited, so to speak, shared space, performed together, collaborated, and lived on common ground. 'Influence' became a function of intermingling, exchange, and collaboration, directly on certain productions, indirectly by imitation. 'Influence' became 'transmission.' The effects of American alternative theatre on the alternative theatre movement in Britain were of multiple types: substantive / thematic, cultural / ideological, aesthetic / technical, and also to a great extent political. Issues of identity operated in all four of these areas.

In effect alternative theatre deconstructed the canonical texts of conventional theatre. Notions of race, character, plot, and act sequence eroded. The collective creative process created contingent, problematised, and to some extent ephemeral productions which challenged actors and audiences to change their culture and society. Alternative theatre broadened the range of subject matter appropriate to and accessible by British theatre audiences. Alternative theatre in Britain and America broadened social discourse and enabled individuals, audiences, and artistic institutions and culture at large to shift views of race, gender, ethnicity, difference, and identity.

Accepted hegemonic identities shifted in response to challenges offered by alternative theatre. Ideologies of power shifted as well and identity became a function of variously composed groups' 'communities'. Individualism was contested as a socio-cultural value as well as a function of national identity. The mutual creation of text and performance revalued the group as a primary entity and collaboration as the expression of human ability.

Two essays, one from 1946, and one from 1967 theorised for literary-critical audiences what alternative theatre could accomplish in fact: Theodor Adorno and Max Horkheimer's *The Culture Industry: Enlightenment as Mass Deception*; and Roland Barthes, *The Death of the Author*. These works provided the intellectual grounding and impetus for many of the changes in approach to text and language evidenced in this book.

Improvisation was the principal technique employed in alternative theatre groups, used to incorporate members of the group into the process of working collectively and creatively (Shank 1972: 4). Through improvisations, work would be built on an initial conception of a new piece, and in many cases the exercises themselves would be developed into the finished performance. Such was the case with the Open Theatre's performances of *The Serpent* (1967) and *Terminal* (1970–1971). Improvisational exercises were utilised by nearly all of American alternative theatre groups during this period, and this creative technique became a characteristic of the new theatre.

At the same time, individual groups developed their own unique methods and exercises based on the specific requirements of a given performance piece. Groups could be distinguished from one another by the means of discovery they employed to develop an idea for a particular piece. For example, the Open Theatre was interested in exploring the work of the actor for its own sake whereas the Living Theatre was not. Alternative theatre groups during this period tended to base the development of their work on exercises which allowed them to respond to a social or political issue, a text, or painting, an object, or material, or from a script generated by someone working within the particular group. Groups were also distinguished by the circumstances of performance (contextuality) within a scenario and whether the scenario did or did not involve spectators.

During the summer of 1967 links with American experimental companies began to spark real change in the British theatrical landscape by introducing new and revolutionary theatre practices. As John Arden noted at the time:

> The summer of 1967 ensured that London had become fully versed in a style of drama which was to characterise much of the city's experimental theatregoing in the next few years (Ansorge 1975: 22).

At the Edinburgh Festival in 1967 the La MaMa Company played four plays at Barry Halls. La MaMa received a lot of attention, especially for *Futz*. Its members met and relaxed at The Traverse (Porter, interview, 2011). The company then transferred to the Vaudeville Theatre in London's West End. During the summer of 1967 the Open Theatre under the direction of Joseph Chaikin performed *America Hurrah* at the Royal Court Theatre. *America Hurrah: Three Views of the U.S.A.* was a trilogy by Jean-Claude van Itallie.

It was necessary for the Royal Court to turn itself into a private club in order to stage the trilogy because the Lord Chamberlain would otherwise have censored the production from public view. In this instance the threat of censorship had the effect of providing free advertising and only served to generate more interest in the production. *America Hurrah* demonstrated how American life is conditioned by ritualistic conventions. At the end of the performance the actors did not emerge and there was no curtain call (van Itallie 1978:143). In doing this the actors challenged an accepted convention of performance even after the performance itself had concluded. This is indicative of an awareness of the potential efficacy of utilising all the ritualistic elements surrounding the performance event even by the act of negating some of them.

Living Theatre

As mentioned in a previous chapter, the couple Judith Malina and Julian Beck (married 1948) set up the Living Theatre in New York in 1947. Over the next thirty years the Living Theatre came to epitomise rebellion against establishment authority and also rebellion against established theatrical conventions. The Living Theatre was originally devoted to poetic drama and the troupe's first public production was Gertrude Stein's *Dr. Faustus Lights the Lights* in 1951 at the Cherry Lane Theatre in Greenwich Village. During the 1950s the Living theatre became increasingly influenced by Brecht and Artaud as well as anarchist theory. In particular Malina, Beck and members of Living Theatre were attracted to the principle of 'drawing the line' which involved taking a stand on a moral point beyond which an individual can no longer be coerced by the power of the state (Tytell 1995: 47).

For years the Living Theatre played to a relatively tiny number of people. Then, within a few weeks of the opening Jack Gelber's *The Connection,* on 15 July 1959, the Living Theatre achieved notoriety and acclaim. The play was about drug dealing, a risky subject, and the play incorporated the presentation of jazz as an integral feature of the production. Jazz and the elements of jazz would also later become indicative of works created by British alternative theatre groups such as the People Show. With *The Connection* the theatre space itself was unexpected, challenging, even disorienting for audiences:

> When you go to *The Connection* in New York you are aware, as you enter the building, of all the denial aspects of the evening. There is no proscenium—(illusion? Well, yes, insofar as the stage is arranged like a squalid room, but it is not like a set; it is more as though the theatre were an extension of the room)—there is no conventional playwriting, no exposition, no development, no story, no characterisation, no construction, and, above all, no tempo. This supreme artifice of the theatre—this one god, whom we all serve, whether in musicals or in melodramas or in the classics—that marvellous thing called pace—is there thrown right out the window. So, with this collection of negative values, you seem to have an evening as boring as life must seem to a young and reluctant devotee sitting on the banks of the Ganges. And yet, if you persevere you are rewarded—from the zero you get to the infinite. (Peter Brook 1987: 27)

The Connection toured to London and played at the Duke of York's in the West End in 1961, bringing to British audiences the experiences Peter Brook described.

Beck and Malina were self-defined radicals who created the Living Theatre to address current political issues. In March 1962

Beck attempted to organise a general strike for peace and participated in a sit-in at Times Square to protest at President Kennedy's resumption of nuclear testing. The police punctured Beck's lung. Joseph Chaikin, who was the lead actor in *The Connection,* was also arrested. The next Living Theatre production was *The Brig* (1963), set in a military prison.

The Internal Revenue Service closed down the Living Theatre during the production of *The Brig,* on 17 October 1963. In 1964, after its base was closed, the Living Theatre left the United States and toured Europe until 1968. Between 1964 and 1968 the Living Theatre was in exile, travelling throughout Europe (Marwick 1998: 343). Their production of *Frankenstein* opened in Venice in September 1965 and led to the company's deportation from Italy. Despite such difficulties—perhaps in some measure because of them—the Living Theatre gained international notoriety and a large following especially among young people.

In 1968 the Living Theatre returned to the United States with a repertory of material which had been created during the period in exile. They first performed four pieces at Yale including *Frankenstein*. Malina and Beck then used the Brooklyn Academy of Music for an audience-involving performance described as 'like a modern Dionysian rite'. *Paradise Now* was perhaps the most extreme example of the Living Theatre's work. *Paradise Now* began with actors circulating among the audience confronting them and denouncing restrictions on their freedom and then openly defying those restrictions. The performance continued for another four or five hours. Actors roamed through the audience, smoking marijuana. First the actors and then some members of the audience tore off their clothes. Judith Malina led the audience out into the Brooklyn streets.

In 1969 the Living Theatre was in London again, based at the Roundhouse. The Roundhouse was originally a Victorian engine shed, located in Chalk Farm, London. The unique dimensions of the Roundhouse soon began to yield interesting artistic experimentation and often determined how work found definition within its cavernous spaces *Paradise Now* deliberately provoked the public into voicing their opposition to the performance itself and then overrode audience protest by shouting obscenities and even sometimes spitting on audience members. Ultimately the Living Theatre sought to move the audience to continue an anarchist revolution. Their aggressive behaviour towards their audiences combined with anarchist politics brought the Living Theatre enormous notoriety. They challenged many long accepted theatrical conventions, as well as conventions of public behaviour.

In particular the Living Theatre posed a challenge to the concept of distinguishing the fictional from the real. The Living Theatre treated space and time as present reality and actors played themselves rather than characters. Actors wore their own clothes and the subject matter was largely drawn from political and social issues of the day. In many cases themes were elucidated through improvised confrontations with the audience rather than by performance of a static and predetermined text. *Paradise Now* was an example of alternative performance deliberately taken to an extreme.

In 1969 the Living Theatre performed four shows in London at the Roundhouse: *Paradise Now*, *Frankenstein*, *Mysteries*, and *Antigone*. Before this the Living Theatre presented *The Connection* (1961) at the Duke of York's in London and *The Brig* (1963) at the Mermaid Theatre. In 1979 the Living Theatre returned to the Roundhouse and performed *Prometheus*. These productions embodied and exemplified many of the influences and effects that this chapter explores.

Open Theatre

Joseph Chaikin began to work with the Living Theatre in 1959. He played roles in Jack Gelber's *The Connection* and in plays by Berthold Brecht, including *In the Jungle of the Cities* and *Man is Man*. He received an Obie award for his performance in *Man is Man* and later received a second Obie award for his role in Brecht's *The Exception and the Rule.* His work on the Brecht plays generated a profound change in Chaikin's outlook as he thought it made clear the shortcomings of Method acting. In working with the Living Theatre he helped to develop experimental approaches to performance in response to and required by the unique aspects of each production.

Unlike the Becks, Chaikin was specifically interested in exploring the actor's craft for its own sake. On 1 February 1963 seventeen actors and four writers met for the first time in an auditorium borrowed from the Living Theatre and formed the new Open Theatre (Bottoms 2004:170). When the Internal Revenue Service closed down the Living Theatre's premises and Living Theatre went into exile in Europe, Chaikin stayed behind to work with the new ensemble.

Chaikin focused on what he believed was essential for the theatre. Open Theatre productions began with work developed through the exploration of contemporaneous role playing theories and theatre games. Such work revolved around the idea of transformation and the constantly shifting reality in which the same performer is able to assume and discard different roles or identities, depending on the context. For Chaikin and the Open Theatre reality was treated not as fixed but as ever-changing. The intended implication was that individuals can reshape themselves and in turn reshape society itself. The work of the Open Theatre sought to reveal the fundamental moral and social patterns hidden beneath troubling contemporary events.

Chaikin had been influenced by Erving Goffman's 1959 book *The Presentation of Self in Everyday Life* and believed in what he referred to as 'the setup'. This was a prescribed role of conventionally defined success dictated for the actor by the existing socio-political system. The Open Theatre workshop experiments had the intention of finding a viable alternative to the kind of emotional exhibitionism which Chaikin thought was intrinsic to the Method tradition and which he believed was used to manipulate the audience.

Through workshops and improvisations Open Theatre actors explored the potential of situations, scenarios and characters. The playwrights working with the Open Theatre would then select and shape those discoveries into a written script. One of the most emblematic and successful examples was *The Serpent* (1967) by Jean-Claude van Itallie in which contemporaneous assassinations of important political figures during the 1960s are interwoven with the biblical story of Adam and Eve.

Another successful Open Theatre collaboration was Megan Terry's *Viet Rock* which ridiculed the bureaucratic justifications for the war in Vietnam and was another collective creation which was a distinctive contribution to theatre of the period. In fact Chaikin employed many female directors and writers, including Megan Terry whose *Viet Rock* was first presented in the spring of 1966 at Cafe La MaMa and Barbara Garson's 1967 *Macbeth* adaptation, *MacBird,* which presented President Johnson as the murderer of John Kennedy.

The goals of the Open Theatre were to redefine the limits of the stage experience, or unfix them. To find ways of reaching each other and the audience. To encourage and inspire playwrights who work with us. To find ways of presenting plays and improvisational programs without the pressures of money, real estate, and other commercial considerations which usurp creative energy. To develop the ensemble (Cole & Chinoy 1970: 664).

With the Open Theatre Chaikin developed what was referred to as the 'transformation exercise'. During the exercise actors were free to respond to the established situation intuitively by transforming themselves physically into an object or an animal or another character. Through this process and through collaboration between the ensemble and playwright Jean-Claude van Itallie, three one-act plays were generated which eventually were presented under the title *America Hurrah* at the Pocket Theatre in May 1966. Although *America Hurrah* shared important characteristics with a number of previous productions this triplet marked a point at which the work of the Open Theatre achieved both commercial success and critical acceptance. *America Hurrah* ran for over a year and, as already noted, toured to London's Royal Court theatre in the summer of 1967. Four years later the Open Theatre returned to London and played at the Roundhouse, a visit organised by Nancy Meckler's husband David Aukin.

La MaMa

The founding of La MaMa in New York's East Village by Ellen Stewart (Marwick 1998: 344) in 1961 changed the course of alternative theatre in America and internationally. Stewart's original aspiration for La MaMa was to provide a venue so that her 'brother', Fred Lights, could have his plays produced. Lights was black so mainstream producers at the time were reluctant to consider his work. Stewart had money from her work as a fashion designer and could afford to hire a basement space on 9th Street in the East Village. She called the space La MaMa.

The venue was tiny and unkempt but Ellen Stewart's initiative ensured that it was full of possibilities, a place where people could come and things could happen. Stewart was told that she could not sell refreshments at La MaMa because she did not have a licence. So Stewart would pass the hat around and those who contributed could come any time during the week to see the show again. Most shows lasted a week. Hot chocolate and instant coffee was served in plastic cups. The actors were paid very little, if anything at all. Stewart was still working for Victor Bijou as a fashion designer and the 'Miss Ellen' label, but, at the same time she was not allowed out on the catwalk when the designs were shared with the public.

Stewart maintained a sewing room next door to the La MaMa space and lived in an apartment upstairs at the premises. Early on neighbours reported her to police as running a brothel when they saw a black woman and white men (playwrights, out-of-work actors) entering the building. Ellen Stewart knew nothing about theatre but thought that, if you did something, it was more fulfilling than sitting around wondering about doing it. There was enough space at La MaMa for a small audience and a bed on stage.

La MaMa existed to provide opportunities for new talent of all types. Initially it remained unsung in Manhattan and unknown elsewhere. When La MaMa had been going for some time Stewart wanted to secure funding. She had been told that she could get a Rockefeller grant if she could accumulate some positive reviews. Stewart could not get the established press to go to the East Village venue so La MaMa first had to tour to Europe to achieve critical recognition (Crespy 2003: 86) if she was to qualify for a Rockefeller grant. The La MaMa tour to Paris in September 1965 turned the enterprise into a celebrated company and the East Village basement into a place of pilgrimage for avant-garde directors from Europe such as Max Stafford-Clark in 1968 and Peter Brook with the RSC in 1971.

La MaMa became a site of artistic transmission. Stafford-Clark's visit, for example, influenced his establishment of the Traverse Workshop Company, according to Ian Brown who worked on its first show in 1970, and, although later Stafford-Clark's aesthetic returned to a more Stanislavskian approach with Joint Stock, the Traverse Workshop Company's successor, his Joint Stock creative method always maintained collaborative methods clearly derived from La MaMa practices.

We will return to the La MaMa tours of Europe after a brief outline of Stafford-Clark's relationship with La MaMa and Off Off Broadway. Max Stafford-Clark was born 17 March 1941 and educated in Felsted, Essex where he won a year's Exchange scholarship to the United States and the Riversdale County Day School in 1958/1959. Stafford-Clark went to Greenwich Village where he saw the first New York City production of *The Zoo Story* by Edward Albee as well as a production of *The Balcony* by Jean Genet. Upon his return to London Stafford-Clark took his father to a number of West End productions including *The Caretaker* by Pinter, *Brand* by Ibsen at the Lyric, Hammersmith, and *The Long and the Short and the Tall* at the Royal Court. Stafford-Clark returned to New York for six weeks in January 1968 to observe and work with La MaMa (Marwick 1998: 351) and worked the follow spot on the original production of *Hair*.

> I stayed with Paul Foster. I operated a follow-spot and I went with Tom O'Horgan down to Philadelphia, where a show was opening. I had access to rehearsals, and I also went while I was there to Nancy Meckler's rehearsals before her arrival in this country. So I was a kind of hanger-on. I was minimally useful. But at that point, having done a bit of work myself, the opportunity to absorb from another director was very important. (Stafford-Clark 2007: 6)

Later Stafford-Clark and the Traverse Workshop Company would emulate La MaMa by having long rehearsal periods (Stafford-Clark, interview, 2009). When Stafford-Clark resigned as Director of the Traverse and set up the Traverse Workshop Company he lived on £6 a week. He would put each single note in six different drawers and the change from each day went back in the drawer. On the seventh day he would live on the remainder. He practiced communal living and lived off a stew that boiled away during the entire week. Despite these circumstances, his ideas were formulating and one major influence on him was Tom O'Horgan and the La MaMa Theatre Troupe from America.

When Stafford-Clark, before setting up the Traverse Workshop Company, was the Traverse Associate Director he had invited La MaMa over to Britain (Stafford-Clark, 2009). La MaMa toured to Britain with *Futz* by Rochelle Owens, *Melodrama Play* by Sam Shepard and *Tom Paine* by Paul Foster. Stafford-Clark admired the fact that the actors also played musical instruments and that Tom O'Horgan was a skilled musicologist. He met Ellen Stewart of La MaMa and respected the physical commitment of La MaMa which was an essential part of their success and dynamism and claims to be influenced by La MaMa the Open Space, Living Theatre, and Jim Haynes as well as 'Happenings' in London.

In 1965 La MaMa toured Europe in two minibuses called Helen and The Star Car. One was purchased for them by the playwright John Arden (Porter, 2011). Their work was receiving largely positive reviews and they had a growing reputation. They rarely stayed in hotels as Ellen Stewart would arrange various places for them to stay. The idea of touring La MaMa productions to Europe coincided with a growing interest in certain American playwrights. Paul Foster's *Hurray for the Bridge* was presented at La MaMa in 1964 and he also worked on a Spanish version which was then staged in Bogota, Colombia, and later at the Festival of Cali. That production generated a booking by a theatre festival in Germany.

The play then gained the notice of the Danish director Jens Okking who had the script translated for a staging in Denmark. Foster and Stewart travelled together to see the production as well as another Foster play staged in Denmark called *The Recluse*. They were greatly impressed by the enthusiastic and sizeable audiences. Another foreign production involving La MaMa artists took place when two regular La MaMa performers, Mary-Claire Charba and Jacque Lynn Colton received praise for their roles in Tom Eyen's *The White Whore and the Bit* at the famous Shakespeare and Co. bookstore in Paris. European audiences and critics at this time were more appreciative of avant-garde theatre than were Americans generally. This convinced Stewart that the critical response abroad would potentially open doors back home for La MaMa and its artists.

Back in New York Stewart activated a plan to return to Europe later in 1965 with a group of actors, directors and playwrights. La MaMa left New York in September 1965 with sixteen La MaMa artists, twenty-two plays, and some props. Stewart selected pieces which she considered to be the best plays La MaMa had produced since 1962. The company was split in two and Tom O'Horgan and Ross Alexander were chosen as directors. According to the plan one company was intended to play in Copenhagen for six weeks and the other in Paris during the same time period. According to the plan after six weeks the two troupes were intended to then switch cities (Bottoms 2004:195).

Circumstances intervened. The Living Theatre had recently played to hostile audiences in Paris. Ross Alexander's La MaMa troupe encountered similar problems and returned to New York prematurely. Tom O'Horgan's troupe, however, received a more positive response and met with receptive audiences in Copenhagen, then Paris. The O'Horgan's troupe returned to Denmark from Paris for an extended engagement. The plays included *Chicago* by Sam Shepard, *This is the Rill Speaking* by Lanford Wilson, *The Recluse* by Paul Foster, *Thank You, Miss Victoria* by William Hoffman, *Birdbath* by Leonard Melfi, *The Circus* by Gerald Shoenwolf, and *War* and *America Hurrah* by Jean-Claude van Itallie.

Although the O'Horgan La MaMa group enjoyed a strong European reception with audiences and critics, in certain ways touring was a difficult experience for the troupe. From the first performance in Paris (at the American Centre for the Arts) there were problems with audience reactions to unconventional material. David Davies, who headed the Centre, was offended by *America Hurrah* which featured masks and life-size puppets designed by Robert Wilson. During the course of the play the figures destroyed a hotel room while scribbling profanity on its walls. Davies gave the troupe twenty-four hours to pack up and leave after the performance. La MaMa left Paris and headed immediately for Denmark.

Stewart, now desperate to keep expenses down, convinced the French railroad to let her travel in freight with the *America Hurrah* puppets, thereby avoiding a passenger fare. In Copenhagen, by contrast, the troupe received, as noted above, a warm reception from established Danish theatre critics. The Danish press considered the troupe to be full of energy and passion but short on acting training and professional technique. Even though the performances were evaluated as amateur the plays were given serious consideration and La MaMa was invited back for two more tours in 1966. These tours took the troupe back to Denmark, Sweden, Yugoslavia, and England.

Tom O'Horgan and his work with La MaMa

Ellen Stewart kept La MaMa's basement space when she moved the troupe to a venue over a laundrette. The La MaMa workshops run by Tom O'Horgan, who was heavily influenced by 'Happenings', were doing things that were not being done anywhere else at the time. O'Horgan was a trained musician and incorporated musical elements into his work. He had a large collection of musical instruments and could play all of them proficiently. His workshop ideas, amongst others, were somewhat inspired by a recent book written about work being done to facilitate the development of autistic children, based on the theory that autistic children often missed out on the crawling stage (Porter, 2011). When movements associated with crawling were produced in autistic children by external manipulation, notable results occurred. O'Horgan became interested in exploring non-verbal theatre. Equally important, O'Horgon had written operas. He wanted to direct his eclectic ideas towards the theatre. He believed that theatre is what happens in the communion or kinetic connection between the actors and the audience.

O'Horgan's ideas resonated with Ellen Stewart's aspirations. He had rejected the predictability of conventional theatre and wanted to create something else. Stewart looked for plays that lent themselves to the kind of exploration that Tom O'Horgan was interested in. For example, originally *Hair* was not initially planned or staged as the innovative phenomenon ultimately created through O'Horgan's vision. Together Stewart and O'Horgan felt that theatre could achieve what other forms of performance, such as ballet, could not achieve because theatre can draw many disciplines together.

Paul Foster, who wrote *Tom Paine,* also believed in this vision. Foster had been with Stewart from the beginning and was enthusiastic about O'Horgan's approach. At the time that the European tour was about to depart Foster had only written Part 1 of *Tom Paine.* Foster accompanied La MaMa to Europe and worked on the script in Denmark where La MaMa had a major fan base. At the time La MaMa was crossing tours in Europe with the Grotowski troupe and the Living Theatre. Also in their rep was *Futz* by Rochelle Owens which was about a farmer's passion for one of his pigs.

Owens was initially resistant to O'Horgan's approach of creating a mini-chorus through workshops on the production but it proved a very effective device. By the time La MaMa returned to Edinburgh from Paris *Tom Paine* was completed. The producers at the Churchill Theatre in Edinburgh arranged a transfer to the Vaudeville Theatre in London. There is a moment in the play when the action stops and audience members are invited to come up on to the stage and contribute their dialogue in the spirit of Tom Paine by not being passive or restricted. The production celebrated the questioning of orthodox ideas at the time (Marowitz 1973: 133–134).

Triumph: Hair

Hair: The American Tribal Love-Rock Musical (1967) by Galt MacDermot, Gerome Ragni, and James Rado is referred to throughout this book but given the topic of this study it is germane to discuss specifically its impact in Britain. Joseph Papp was an important advocate for free public theatre beginning with the establishment of the New York Shakespeare Festival in 1954. Papp established the Public Theatre in 1967 with the intention of imitating the London branch of the Royal Shakespeare Company in putting on contemporary productions aimed at an audience comprised of a large cross-section of society. The Public Theatre opened on 29 October 1967 with *Hair: The American Tribal Love-Rock Musical.*

After an initial run *Hair* continued to play at a midtown Manhattan discotheque, then was retooled and transferred to the Biltmore on Broadway in 1968 (Wollman 2006: 42). The production was completely restructured by La MaMa director Tom O'Horgan. Papp did not prioritise pleasing conventional middle-class Broadway audiences with his work but rather he was interested in connecting with the younger generation who were concerned with contemporary issues and changing society. At the time Britain offered an example for Papp of the way in which theatrical innovation advanced across a broad front in the new civic theatres which were essentially a legacy of the war.

On 26 September 1968 the new Theatres Act removed the Lord Chamberlain's licensing provision from the statute books. The next day *Hair*, directed by O'Horgan, opened at the Shaftesbury Theatre in London. Many within the alternative theatre movement regarded the production as a betrayal and a commercial sell-out (Bottoms 2004: 210–213). Nonetheless *Hair* originated in the experimental realm of Off Off Broadway theatre in New York. In preparation for the production Tom O'Horgan adopted an old tactic used at Café Cino of searching the streets of New York, looking for people he believed looked right for the piece and inviting them to audition.

Hair posited radical themes, including anti-Vietnam sentiment, free love, L.S.D., communal living, and racial and sexual equality. Performances of *Hair* were adjusted and localised to fit the particular communities in which they took place which was also the case with the London production. In many communities the production was besieged by bomb scares and death threats (Johnson 2004:124) but nonetheless at the end of each performance the audience was still encouraged to come up on stage and commune with the cast through song and dance. As Charles Marowitz observed,

Every so often a show comes along which consolidates some part of the zeitgeist and whose significance is less in what it is than the time at which it arrives, and in the face of such a show, drama criticism suddenly appears like a gross impertinence because one can no sooner review the Present than attempt to evaluate the latitude and longitude of one's native city. *Hair* is such a show. It is the cohesion of a dozen contemporary trends, the most dominant of which is hip-culture, drug-enthusiasms, the Cage concept of Indeterminacy, and the Marcusian theory of protest. Coming as the first blast after the Lord Chamberlain's demise, it has properly shook up London-town (Marowitz 1973: 142).

This comment is emblematic of a micro/macro parallel to be made regarding the generation of alternative theatre in Britain examined in this book. In a sense an individual instance of performance such as the London premiere of *Hair* is a microcosm of contemporaneous life. It encompasses both the individual experience as well as providing a prism for contemporaneous events and trends. The individual and collective impetus of theatre practitioners combined, reflected, and reinforced changes taking place in British culture and society.

We now look in depth at a one-time assistant to Tom O'Horgan who forged a bridge between Off Off Broadway and British alternative theatre.

Beth Porter and London La MaMa

Beth Porter was born in New York City on 23 May 1942. She attended Bard College in upstate New York, then transferred to Hunter College in the city. Hunter College was a progressive university in the early 1960s and participated in events which marked socio-cultural shifts at the time. In Greenwich Village at the time you could walk down the street and meet the likes of Bob Dylan, before the pressures of fame and celebrity took hold. (Porter, 2011). Andy Warhol used to frequent The Dom, the American equivalent of a Working Men's Club. Warhol used this as his stomping ground and later established 'The Factory' there to make what he was doing more publicly available. Beth Porter went to The Dom for the delicious, cheap food (Porter, 2011).

'Happenings' took place in lofts and little theatres at the time, events not frequented by or recognised by the establishment. Beth Porter met people like Allen Ginsberg and Robert Frank with whom she made a film called *Me and My Brother*. Apart from writers for the *Village Voice,* no reviewers passed below 14th Street. This theatre activity was radical: it subverted the norms, geographical as much as aesthetic, of established New York theatre.

Hunter College, one of the University of N.Y.C. colleges, enrolled only women at the time. It had a reputation for its theatre, theatre criticism, and history of art courses. The woman running the theatre department was named Vera Mowry. Mowry mounted a production of *Othello* featuring Beth Porter as Emilia. Mowry searched Off Off Broadway looking for out-of-work actors to bring in for her productions. One such actor was Neil Flannagan who was with Caffe Cino, and Michael Warren-Powell who at the time was Lanford Wilson's lover. Wilson came to see *Othello* and later took Porter to meet Ellen Stewart at La MaMa's new venue on 2nd Avenue (Porter, 2011).

Stewart was producing Wilson's play, *The Rimers of Eldritch,* and Wilson wanted Porter to be in it. Stewart agreed. Porter played opposite Fred Forrest while the La MaMa prototype troupe, under the direction of Tom O'Horgan, was touring in Europe. Porter found Stewart to be unexpectedly beautiful and extremely down-to-earth (Porter, 2011). Stewart believed in her instincts and wanted to make things happen for people she believed in. She completely changed Porter's life (Porter, 2011). Stewart allowed Porter to have experiences she had never expected to have, including forming the Warehouse La MaMa in London. Stewart introduced Porter to Tom O'Horgan She was then cast in *East Bleecker* by Jack Micheline, playing a Mexican whore. Stewart still wanted to gather a reliable and good troupe together in order to secure the Rockefeller grant and wanted new blood and expertise to assist her. Beth Porter was invited to join La MaMa and to do workshops with Tom O'Horgan.

Prior to the company going to Brandeis University in Waltham, Massachusetts, Porter became ill and had to stay behind in New York where she was cared for by Harvey Milk and his then partner, Jack Galen McKinley (Porter, 2011). She became O'Horgan's assistant (O'Horgan was also assisted by Cameron Mackintosh). Working with O'Horgan made it possible for Porter to go to England and ultimately set up her own company. She approached Stewart to say that she would like to set up a La MaMa company in Europe. Originally Porter did not want the new troupe to be London-based as she wanted it to be a touring company and nomadic. Porter did not want a director since she thought O'Horgan would be irreplaceable and wanted the troupe to be a creative collective instead (Porter, 2011). Stewart agreed but said they could not take the La MaMa label until they had proved themselves. It was at this time Max Stafford-Clark was attending La MaMa workshops and taking notes on their methods of work.

During the London production of *Hair*, Porter, along with other performers and O'Horgan, all shared a flat while rehearsing at Shaftesbury Theatre. Porter ran some of the rehearsal workshops for the show as did the Beatles' friend and collaborator Victor Spinetti who was a Tony-winning actor, a product of Joan Littlewood's Stratford East Theatre Workshop, and later star of Jane Arden's *Vagina Rex and the Gas Oven* at the Drury Lane Arts Lab in 1969. Porter got to know Spinetti and was invited to his parties. There was a sense of community. Porter's group was making their own theatre and looking for a place to discover and perform. Porter rang around to people she met during that year and all of them were encouraging and helpful (Porter, 2011).

Wherehouse La MaMa (1968–1972)

Jim Haynes had recently opened the Arts Lab on Drury Lane in August of 1967 and let Porter's La MaMa group work in the space for free. Wherehouse La MaMa developed its work there and did its first presentation at the Drury Lane Arts Lab. Other companies working at the Arts Lab at the time included the Portable Theatre and the People Show. At its inception The Wherehouse Company included: Stephen Rea, Dinah Stabb, Maurice Colbourne, and Nancy Meckler, who had come over from the United States to join them. Porter and Meckler both have differing accounts of the split with Wherehouse La MaMa that lead to the formation of Freehold. I will provide each of their accounts respectively beginning with Porter here and then revisiting Meckler in Chapter Six. Meckler had been a Stage Manager on a number of La MaMa Plexus shows in New York and was an ambitious director. However at the time Porter did not want a director and said that Meckler could only observe and take part in the workshops (Porter, 2011).

The troupe which would formally be named Wherehouse La MaMa presented *Street Piece* (1968) which evolved out of workshop exercises requiring actors to walk at geometric angles and choose whether or not to encounter, verbally or not, the person you met at the corner of your turning. The play was evocative of and about urban life. The actors also performed the witches' scene from *Macbeth* in O'Horgan's style, using a strange cacophony of sounds and a varying number of witches. Another piece was *Mr Jello* (1968) by George Bernissa, which had been given to the group by Stewart (Porter, 2011). It was about the disappointments of personal relationships but was also comical, weird, and liberating for the actors and audience. Actors worked without a director trying to put into practice what they had learnt from O'Horgan. *Mr. Jello* was presented at the Drury Lane Arts Lab.

Stewart was supporting the new troupe's actors financially during this time, combining assets she contributed with the box-office earnings to support the troupe. There was not a lot of money available but the first 10% of anything went towards administration, props, and other expenses and the rest was divided equally amongst the company (Porter, 2011). Because of the reviews the troupe received Ellen Stewart then allowed Porter's company to take the name of The Wherehouse La MaMa and as such it also became known as London La MaMa. Its patrons were Victor Spinetti, Ellen Stewart, and Anthony Shaffer the English playwright, novelist, and screenwriter.

After appearing in the stage version of *Futz,* Beth Porter was asked to act in the film version of *Futz* (1969) which was shooting in California in 1968, produced by Ben Shapiro and Alan Stroh. Porter had to fly out for the filming of *Futz* but, according to Porter, before she left some of the actors complained about the way Nancy Meckler had been treating them (Porter, 2011). According to Porter, upon her return from California, she arrived at the usual rehearsal space to find that Meckler had taken over the company and the rehearsals, saying that Porter could not expect to be just slotted back in after having left for her film shoot. Porter said that Meckler could not take over the company and so Meckler left with some of the actors to form what later became known as Freehold.

Wherehouse La MaMa presented a play at the Brighton Combination and Porter was joined by Cindy Oswin, Dave Webster, and his wife, Jean Michaelson. Neil Hornick, from Phantom Captain, joined them a little later on. Tours in Europe were booked, along with festivals, and publicity was sent out. Wherehouse La Mama had a rehearsal space in Gerrard Street which they also hired out. They presented *Street Pieces* and *Witches* (1968) and were evolving a piece called *Group Juice* (1968) at the same time (Porter, 2011). *Group Juice* was a very physical piece and Wherehouse La MaMa tended not to write things down so there were hardly any scripts.

During the performance of *Group Juice* the audience came into the theatre and the actors were standing around talking. Then the actors formed themselves into a line and the audience members were enjoined to stand by whomever they wanted. The actor with the longest line of people became the piece's protagonist (Porter,

2011). The play was intended to be like a journey through life, involving birth, education, army training, action, and death. The play was non-intellectual, very physical and startling in that nothing else quite like it was being done at that time in Britain. In rehearsals the actors would take turns being the 'eye', standing outside the action and shaping the performance. This brought a particular cohesion and feel to the work (Porter, 2011).

Wherehouse La MaMa also produced *The Hilton Keynes Blow Your Chances Top of the Heap Golden Personality Show of the Week* (1969). This piece was developed because Neil Hornick who had an academic background, was interested in psychology and psychosexuality, and had read a book on self-mutilation or body mutilation (Porter, 2011). The impetus for the performance piece was the idea that a confrontation with such difficult themes combined with the potential efficacy of performance creates the possibility to reshape identity.

Wherehouse La MaMa also found themselves disappointed with British television in general as it seemed to be influenced by American commercialism and entertainment. Quiz shows placed a monetary value on knowledge. So they took the idea to a comic extreme knowing they would shock British audiences and produced their own 'quiz show' (Porter, 2011). The quiz show was run by Hilton Keynes (Roy Martin), whose name combines the commercialism of the hotel chain and the bureaucratic planning control embedded in the British new town Milton Keynes, in a glitzy tuxedo and his lovely assistant Jean Michaelson who was in fact nine months pregnant. The actors went into the audience posing as drug police to root out drugs in the audience. Beth Porter was planted in the audience as a volunteer. Having worked and learned from O'Horgan they were all physically agile. The encounter with Porter turned into an acrobatic act. At the end they were applauded by the audience, then used an APPLAUD sign as in a stereotypical recording studio.

The performance included a talent act involving the Royal Family dressed in costumes and masks as well as a saxophone-playing corgi. There was also a 'Memory Man' in an enclosed booth answering questions. If he got a question wrong, gas was poured into the booth. The final question was how many Jews were killed in the war? Answers began with '300?' and gas poured into the booth. The Memory Man tried again, but every time he got the answer wrong more gas poured into the booth until the man was dead. These constructions amounted to the 'acts' of the play. Irving Wardle nominated Porter as the most promising actress of the year in *The Times* (Porter, 2011).

Wherehouse La MaMa presented the show at The Place courtesy of a contact with the leading Martha Graham dancer, Robert Cohan, who was based at The Place and because a company member had designed the original seating for the venue (Porter, 2011). Wherehouse La MaMa went on to play at the Newcastle Festival, Edinburgh and then went on tour in Europe. People who saw the show would ring up the company and invite them to come to their festivals. Porter would negotiate on the phone by asking for costs to cover travel, board, food, and company wages which had to be in cash as they had no bank account (Porter, 2011).

Ellen Stewart invited Wherehouse La MaMa to perform in New York. Before that she paid for, in London, the production of William Hoffman's, a La MaMa playwright's play, *XX XXX*, subtitled *A Nativity Play* (1970), which Wherehouse performed at Marowitz's Open Space. The critic Harold Hobson hated it so much that he suggested the Arts Council should discontinue its funding. Wherehouse had a falling out with Thelma Holt at the Open Space. Holt, according to Porter, then refused to pay them. According to

Porter there was an uneasy relationship between Charles Marowitz and Wherehouse La MaMa.

The Wherehouse Company went to New York in 1971 where Stewart was presenting a rotation of other visiting companies at La MaMa, including Theatre of the Ridiculous and The Ridiculous Theatre Company. Stewart asked The Wherehouse Company to align with the Playhouse of the Ridiculous in a presentation of a play called *The Organ Grinder or The Monkey* (1970), presented alongside the other work which they had been developing independently (Porter, 2011). Wherehouse La MaMa provides an example of a direct link between British alternative theatre and an American Off Off Broadway exemplar.

Bread and Puppet

Bread and Puppet also came to Britain and was another influence on British alternative theatre as well as forms of public protest incorporating elements of theatricality. As Kathleen McCreery of Broadside Mobile Workers Theatre stated,

> We learn from today's filmmakers, from groups such as Bread and Puppet, from dancers, musicians, journalists, and from other theatre groups. We are continually experimenting with new forms. (Itzin 1980: 241)

The early training of Peter Schumann, born in Germany in 1934, was in the sculptural arts. He arrived in New York at the time of Kaprow's Happenings in 1957 and did his first theatrical work at the Living Theatre. In 1963 he founded the Moosaka Puppet Theatre and then came across the material which made it possible to create the fourteen-foot tall puppets which were to become characteristic of what became known as the Bread and Puppet Theatre. Bread and Puppet Theatre was based in a loft in Delancey Street in lower Manhattan. At the end of performances bread was distributed to the audience. Schumann explained that he and his colleagues named the theatre The Bread and Puppet because they felt that theatre should be as basic as bread.

Bread and Puppet was a pacifist theatre company influenced by the principles of nineteenth-century Romanticism and early Christianity. Its work focused on themes involving the natural environment and the corruption of both nature and man through greed and power. The company saw itself as connected to an ancient art form in puppetry and rejected the Western tradition of literary theatre. Bread and Puppet most often performed in non-traditional spaces and was perhaps best known for its production of *The Cry of the People for Meat* (1969) which involved two twenty-foot tall puppets, including Mother Earth and a sinister Uncle Sam representing the forces of greed and imperialism. The Virgin Mary appeared in many Bread and Puppet productions in the form of a Grey Lady, a sorrowing mother puppet. Other well-known Bread and Puppet pieces included *The Great Warrior* (1963), *A Man Says Goodbye to his Mother* (1966), and *Domestic Resurrection Circus* (1970).

The first Bread and Puppet peace demonstration took place on 3 March 1964 (Marwick 1998: 345–346). Bread and Puppet responded to the beginning of the American bombing of North Vietnam in February 1965 with the Greenwich Village Puppet Parade, March 1965. In April 1965 Bread and Puppet participated in a March on Washington to end American involvement in Vietnam. Bread and Puppet participated in several anti-Vietnam War demonstrations in America but also in Britain. In a march in New York in November 1966 Bread and Puppet marched with Allen Ginsberg while a sound-truck played music by the Supremes and the Beatles.

Artistic recognition in America for the Bread and Puppet Theatre came with the production of *Fire* in 1966. *Fire* was the first of three plays dealing directly with Vietnam. In one sense artistic recognition was a form of success. But even when the company was invited to perform at the World Theatre Festival at Nancy in April 1968 Schumann maintained an unbending rejection of worldly success. To be interested in success or even modest success was frowned upon within the company. In Britain Bread and Puppet collaborated with Ed Berman and Inter-Action and also appeared at the Royal Court in 1969. In fact, they have been widely celebrated and are singled out as icons of the 1960s and the anti-Vietnam protest movement.

Conclusion

Collectively the American based groups discussed in this chapter were responsible for a surge of creativity and the injection of new practices, ideas, and ways of generating theatre in Britain. The influence of the four major American groups which toured Britain during the 1960s and 1970s on the landscape of British alternative theatre was critical. This influence would serve to broaden the horizons of theatre practice in Britain and its engagement with British society.

During this period there were several anti-Vietnam war protest marches in Britain, many of which involved a certain level of theatricality and included such groups as Bread and Puppet. Peter Brook's production of *US* at the Aldwych Theatre in 1966 challenged the American involvement in Vietnam. During the rehearsal process for *US* Brook and the RSC consulted with both Susan Sontag and Joseph Chaikin (Chambers 2004: 155). In an interview given at the time Brook stated the following:

> *The Royal Shakespeare Theatre* is using public money to do a play about Americans at war in Vietnam. This fact is so explosive, and has brought out so many contradictory reactions, that for once some explanation seems necessary. There are times when I am nauseated by the theatre, when its artificiality appals me, although at the very same moment I recognise that its formality is its strength. The birth of *US* was allied to the reaction of a group of us who quite suddenly felt that Vietnam was more powerful, more acute,

> more insistent a situation than any drama that already existed between covers. (Peter Brook 1987: 61)

The impact of the Off Off Broadway movement on the founding of the Other Place and Warehouse spaces at the Royal Shakespeare Company as well as the theatre upstairs at the Royal Court was important. In *Other Spaces: New Theatre and the RSC* (1980) Colin Chambers details how the establishment of the Other Place and the Warehouse venues at the RSC were influenced by American Off Off Broadway such as the work of La MaMa and Ellen Stewart. In doing this Chambers establishes a link between the experimental practices of the Off Off Broadway movement and a publicly subsidised institution within the British theatre.

Buzz Goodbody, who was responsible for the Warehouse and Other Place venues at the RSC in Stratford-upon-Avon, also worked at Charles Marowitz's Open Space Theatre. Marowitz's assistant at the Open Space, the American Walter Donahue was the Literary Manager of the Other Place. As we have noted, the RSC also visited La MaMa in New York in 1971 when the company was officially in New York to perform Peter Brook's famous production of *A Midsummer Night's Dream* at the Brooklyn Academy of Music (Chambers, 2011).

In concluding this chapter, it may help to provide one clear final example of the sort of American influence on alternative theatre practice in Britain during this period. The Pip Simmons Group was founded at the Drury Lane Arts Lab in 1968 and combined social commentary with a physical theatre mode of performance, although interestingly Simmons himself did not go to the United States until 1973. The Group's main body of work was based on representations of American culture and society. Its production of *Superman* (1969), for example, was inspired by American culture, based on a real life comic book in which Superman becomes involved in the Civil Rights Movement. In the play Superman is the star of a TV talk show. He delivers theories about the reasons for different social problems but in a cartoon style with the sort of dialogue one would find in a comic-book bubble.

Equally important, the Pip Simmons Group's production of *Do It!* (1971) was about the student protests and the violent police reaction to them at the 1968 Democratic Convention in Chicago, described in a subsequent Walker Report as a 'police riot' (Walker 1968: 1, 10–11).

The first half was an attempt to recreate the 1968 riots in the auditorium…At one point during *Do It!* The Yippies threw faeces into the faces of the Pentagon guards and then proceeded to run hysterically through the audience demanding support for their actions. Simmons once described to me the reaction during a performance at Southampton University…At Southampton it took about five minutes for the audience to get the message. Then one actor screamed "Come on! You can't all be pigs!" and about thirty people joined the actors running through the audience. It was like a madhouse (Ansorge 1975: 30).

There was an ideological transaction as the performance challenged the fundamental constitution of the audience's community identity. The perceived ideological meaning of the performance was directly influenced by the particular context in which the performance took place. At the heart of much of the company's work was an attack on mainstream liberal values.

The Group's next production was *The George Jackson Black and White Minstrel Show* (1973), based on minstrel shows which historically were wildly popular in the American South. Towards the end of the first half a mock slave auction was held, into which the company incorporated the audience.

> The audience were deliberately lured into the snares of racial thinking. Towards the end of the first half a slave auction was held. The minstrels ran through the audience begging to be bought. The purpose was to evoke a

> direct response from the audience... I watched several people in the audience ask their slaves to buy them drinks; a few gave them their freedom. They had accepted the false vocabulary of a master-slave relationship. (Ansorge 1975: 34)

The direct link between developing alternative practice in British theatre and its American models could perhaps not be more clearly demonstrated.

We turn now to four American practitioners of alternative theatre during the period 1956–1980 whose seminal work occasioned, tested and encoded alternative American theatre practices in British contexts. Our goal is to analyse the contributions of each individually as well as collectively to alterations in culture, identity, and performance efficacies, and to assess the contribution each made to the history of influence traced above.

Chapter Four: Jim Haynes

This chapter explores the contribution Jim Haynes made to British theatre and British culture more generally starting in 1956 when he was first stationed at a US military installation outside of Edinburgh, Scotland. According to Haynes, he does not believe in the concept of art, strictly speaking. In his view art is just information which some people write, others perform, and others play. For him art is all based on imagination and experience. A child's drawing to him is as important as a Rembrandt (Haynes, 2011, David Weinberg Interview Collection). Haynes, from Louisiana, was a key founder of the Traverse Theatre in Edinburgh in 1963 and the Arts Lab on Drury Lane in 1967. These experimental venues were immensely important seedbeds and catalysts for theatrical change and innovation on both technical and aesthetic levels. It is useful to consider Haynes's history before considering the venues and publications he started.

Haynes was born in Haynesville, Louisiana, on 10 November 1933. Haynes was born coincidentally in the same parish as Ellen Stewart, the founder of La MaMa. His memories of his early years in a Southern town are that he was always out of step with the racism he claims to have fought whenever it appeared, even from an early age. Haynes read his father's books, including Langston Hughes's *I Too Sing America* and Dorothy Parker's poetry which had an early effect on him (Haynes, 2009, Unfinished Histories). His father was in the oil business in Venezuela and when Haynes was thirteen years old, the family moved there. Haynes lived in Venezuela for two years (1946–1948) and attended an international school there which had small class sizes. At the end of two years his parents elected to send him to the Georgia Military Academy in Atlanta where he stayed for three years before enrolling at Louisiana

State University. At the military boarding school he was at the top of his class and ran a literary society (Haynes, 2009, UH). He travelled between the United States and Venezuela repeatedly. This made him early on, he claims, a world traveller and contributed to his dreams, aspirations, and hopes. Haynes first saw theatre locally in Shreveport, Louisiana, and Off Broadway productions when he went to New York. He remembers seeing *Porgy and Bess, South Pacific*, and *The Threepenny Opera* with Lotte Lenya (Haynes, 2009, UH) on Broadway.

Haynes joined the Air Force in 1955 as a Russian language specialist. He was stationed at Kirknewton Air Force Base outside of Edinburgh where he saw his first Edinburgh Festival Fringe production in 1956: Ugo Betti's *Corruption in the House of Justice* by the Oxford University Dramatic Society at the Moray House Theatre in the Royal Mile. Haynes's job was to monitor Soviet radio transmissions. Therefore his very presence in the UK was a direct consequence of military links between the US and Britain, the 'special relationship' described by Churchill and solidified because of the Cold War. At that time the Fringe was very small, involving around thirty companies. He met Richard Demarco and his wife and sister there and they became life-long friends. That evening they also attended a late night production of Italian mime at a venue in Tollcross and Haynes went back with the Demarcos to their place and talked until breakfast (Demarco, 2011).

After Haynes was discharged from the US Air Force he opened the Paperback Bookshop in Charles Street, in the middle of Edinburgh University's city campus, in 1959, whose presence was famously marked by the head of a rhinoceros which hung outside it. The bookshop appears to have been the first to specialise in paperback books in Britain. After he finished in the military his parents wanted him to return home and train as a lawyer, however he wanted to stay in Edinburgh and therefore he was financially on his own. He sold his car to buy the freehold of a junk shop for £300 so that he could open the bookshop. He had no problems staying in Edinburgh after leaving the US Air Force because Britain allowed people to stay if they generated money and employed people. He had permanent residency in Britain from 1959 onward. Haynes wrote to bookshops and publishers all over Britain, saying that he was starting a bookshop next to the University which would sell only paperback books. According to Haynes contacts in Scandinavia provided him with books that were out of print in Britain. The area's original buildings are now demolished and replaced by the modern buildings of the University's Department of Informatics, outside which a statue of a rhinoceros head and a plaque commemorates the former presence of the Paperback Bookshop on that site. The Bookshop comprised two small rooms on the main floor, together with a basement and a basement gallery.

Local sculptors and tapestry makers used the gallery, the first of its type in Edinburgh. Haynes gave out free tea and coffee to those visiting the bookshop and stocked books that were banned elsewhere. He became friends with an English language publisher in Paris, Maurice Girodias, who, in 1953, had started Olympia Press which specialised in erotic writing. Girodias provided books to Haynes such as Frank Harris's *My Life and Loves,* Henry Miller's *Tropic of Cancer,* Lawrence Durrell's *The Black Book, The Ginger Man* by J.P. Donleavy, and many other titles not available elsewhere.

In 1960, after the famous trial under the Obscene Publications Act of 1959 which allowed Penguin to publish *Lady Chatterley's Lover,* Haynes started selling the book in his Paperback Bookshop. One day a retired missionary, Agnes Cooper, purchased a copy of the book and removed it from the bookshop using a pair of coal tongs. She proceeded to set the book on fire while yelling at gathering bystanders. Haynes called Richard Demarco who captured the incident in a photograph. The event was then widely reported in the media throughout the UK and internationally. Haynes received letters of support from many people, including the founder of Penguin, Allen Lane.

The bookshop was used for signings, concerts, and performances. The first of these occasions took place in 1960, and Haynes dates the journey of the Traverse Theatre from this point onward. The first production was a stage adaptation of David Hume's *Dialogues Concerning Natural Religion,* (Haynes 1984: 41). The production involved two actors dressed as eighteenth-century scholars, drinking claret, smoking pipes, and discussing philosophy. In *The Sunday Times* Harold Hobson described the Edinburgh Festival production as the best thing in town, at the best venue, during August 1960. The bookshop held sixty people, sitting on benches. Tea and coffee were served after the performance and audiences were invited to stay and discuss the play.

Traverse Theatre

According to Haynes the founding of the Traverse theatre was the story of two love affairs (Haynes, 2009, UH). A man called Tom Mitchell came to know an MA student at Edinburgh University named Tamara Alferoff whom Haynes already knew from taking classes at Edinburgh University. Tamara Alferoff introduced Haynes to Mitchell. Mitchell began buying properties in Edinburgh and one of these was a building in James Court, off the Lawnmarket, the section of the Royal Mile nearest the Castle, a building which became the Traverse. Originally Mitchell was going to turn it into flats but instead Haynes persuaded him to let him rent it for one shilling a week to use as a theatre. The second love affair was that of Haynes and Jane Alexander. During the summer of 1960 Haynes met a woman named Jane Quigley who later became a famous actress known as 'Jane Alexander'. (During the Clinton administration, Jane Alexander became the American equivalent of

Britain's Minister for the Arts.) In 1960 Quigley was at the Festival playing in Tennessee William's *Orpheus Descending*. Haynes became an offstage voice in the production. After Quigley returned to the United States, Haynes set about planning a theatre for her to play when she came back to Edinburgh. Ironically Jane Alexander never did play at the Traverse. Alferoff and Alexander inspired the establishment of the Traverse but neither is now remembered for this. Haynes believes that photos of both should hang in the Traverse bar.

Haynes set up the Traverse with the help and active participation of Demarco, John Calder (the publisher who championed avant-garde literature and writers such as Samuel Beckett), and John Martin, a local graphic designer who put money in and did early graphic designs for the theatre. There were also many others who helped 'white wash the fences' to make it happen. *In Praise of Joy: White-Washing Fences* (Mosaic Press) is the title of Haynes's 2005 book, a title which describes his way of getting things done. Haynes took the title from the famous fence-painting episode in *The Adventures of Tom Sawyer* about finding a way to persuade people to join in and help in getting things up and running for free. Haynes did exactly that with the coffee shop and the theatre.

The Traverse Theatre Club was formed in the autumn of 1962 with a constitution and the objective that the club should present serious theatre productions of the type not usually presented for economic reasons, and, in general, for the encouragement of Scottish and other music, poetry, pottery, sculpture, painting, books, and art. Haynes established the Traverse under Scots Law and every member of the club was a part-owner. There was a board and an annual general meeting where, every year from 1960 to 1966 Haynes would be made Chair until he chose to step down.

The Traverse Theatre Club opened on 2 January 1963 with a double bill of Arrabal's *Orison* and a production of Jean-Paul Sartre's *Huis Clos* but during the second performance of the Sartre play the actress Colette O'Neill was accidentally stabbed with a paper knife and seriously wounded. Fortunately she recovered but there was publicity as a consequence of the incident. Shortly before the opening of the Traverse Haynes's son Jesper was born to his then wife Viveka. With the exception of a short excursion to the United States with his new born son Jesper and his then wife Viveka, Haynes was involved in all aspects of the theatre's work, all of the time. From Haynes's perspective the bar, gallery, and restaurant were just as important as the theatre in creating a space for social interaction. 'Talk Outs' were held in the theatre, for example, where controversial local topics were debated. Major exhibitions were held in the gallery managed by Demarco, who was also vice-chairman of the management committee. Profits to be used in the theatre came from the bar, restaurant, gallery, and membership. The Traverse created a particular school of Scottish playwrights thereby creating a space for the contestation of Scottish national identity. One of the first to come through was the Glaswegian C.P. Taylor, whose 1980 masterwork *Good*, was premiered by the RSC and was then produced in the West End and on Broadway. Because the Traverse was a club there were no problems with the Lord Chamberlain or censorship and the Traverse could also serve food and drink on Sundays. At one point the Traverse had a grant from the Festival Society which allowed it to pay artists a little more, but generally it paid Equity minimum, £15 per week. According to the website 'Measuring Worth' the modern value of 15 pounds is £257. New work received critical acclaim, the actors got notices and the potential for both made playwrights and actors want to work there.

Connections

Haynes knew the publisher John Calder in London through his ownership of the Paperback Bookshop. Calder knew Charles Marowitz and the director Michael Geliot and introduced both to Haynes. Haynes then involved Geliot, the established Scottish actor and director Callum Mill (Callum Mill was the Artistic Director of the Citizens' Theatre 1960–1962 where he staged an international repertoire), and Marowitz with the Traverse. Mill encouraged Haynes who was learning on the job and also brought in a Scottish angle. Marowitz had presented his Theatre of Cruelty season with Peter Brook at LAMDA which Haynes had seen. Haynes and Marowitz got on well and a lifelong friendship ensued although Marowitz was not always the most diplomatic of directors. Together they brought in guest directors, actors and new plays.

A lot went on at the Traverse during Festival time. During the early 1960s few places were open for people to drink and eat late at night and on Sundays, so the Traverse was a place people went to. The Paperback Bookshop used to sell tickets for performances, and productions continued there even after Haynes sold it on. Haynes produced the first Fringe programme in 1960 and got companies presenting work at the theatre to commit to advertising in the pages of the programme, a model that continues to this day.

It is also worth noting that Richard Demarco was in communication with Ellen Stewart of La MaMa during the formative period in the history of the Traverse and Stewart helped and encouraged the efforts of Haynes and Demarco in Edinburgh (Demarco, May 2011). Under Haynes's directorship the intention was to perform exclusively new plays and preferably those with an unconventional structure, although this was not immediately the reality in practice. The programme for the first six months included the plays already mentioned as well as *Two for the See-Saw* by William Gibson, *Fairy Tales of New York* by J.P. Donleavy, Arrabal's *Picnic in the Battle-Field*, and *Fando and Lis*, Shaw's *Don Juan in Hell*, Jarry's *Ubu Roi*, Ibsen's *A Doll's House*, Ionesco's *The Lesson*, Genet's *The Maids*, Coward's *Private Lives*, and *Requiem for a Nun* by William Faulkner (McMillan 1988: 105–106). Plays by Saul Bellow, Samuel Beckett, Heathcote Williams, and many others later premiered at the Traverse (Haynes 1984: 51–57).

The Traverse collaborated with the La MaMa Troupe in New York and was responsible for the transfer of ground-breaking experimental American productions, mentioned in previous chapters, such as *Futz* by Rochelle Owens and *Tom Paine* by Paul Foster to Britain in 1967. By common consent the Traverse was a bohemian enclave in what was then a run-down working-class area surrounded by a very middle-class and generally hostile city. There can be no doubt that the Traverse challenged and, in time, changed prevailing social and cultural values, at first in Edinburgh and Scotland, but very soon through its influence, led in its first years by Haynes, throughout the rest of Britain.

In 1962 John Calder, Sonia Orwell and Jim Haynes, set up *The Novel Today* conference. Conference participants were on stage together for a whole week at Edinburgh University's dedicated graduation hall, McEwan Hall. Parties took place every night and the Conference was also part of the official Festival. In September 1963, again in McEwan Hall, Haynes, Calder, and Kenneth Tynan organised the first International Drama Conference. One hundred and twenty international theatre artists attended, including Peter Brook, Sir Laurence Olivier, Ionesco, and Martin Esslin (Marowitz 1990: 55). In other words, the Traverse was associated with challenging ideas in what was then a rather conservative city. During a scheduled speech at the 1963 conference Marowitz set out to codify a rigid interpretation of Beckett's *Waiting for Godot*. He insisted that his should be the official interpretation of *Godot*, no flexibility or alternatives allowed. Although clearly intended as satire, Marowitz's provocation set a chain of events in motion which resulted, on the last day of the conference, in what is widely considered to be the very first 'Happening' in the UK.

A "Happening" is a collective experience, based on chance, surrealism, Dada, non-narrative theatre and the Zen Huang Po doctrine of universal mind which held that 'centricity within each event is not dependant on other events' (Aronson 2000:38). For this, Marowitz, Allan Kaprow, and a number of collaborators were responsible. Kaprow had earlier coined the term 'Happening' during the spring of 1959 in New York and had since become a well-known practitioner. The 'Happening' was a deliberate attempt to generate performance crisis and subvert and replace dominant post-Renaissance theatre and Western theatrical conventions dating back to Aristotle. In this case, it included a nude woman being wheeled across a gallery space. Although at the time women could appear nude on the British stage as long as they did not move, pictures on the front pages of the national press depicted nudity in motion and it caused a scandal. The 'Happening' itself was received with great outrage by many of the attenders. Nevertheless, it provoked important questions about performance consciousness and what was 'real' and what was 'not real'. Essential questions were posited concerning time and the collective versus individual experience of performance (Marowitz 1990:66).

The 'Happening' was a deliberate attack on the conference participants' fundamental sense of what is theatrical. In most traditional theatre the play is understood through a cumulative reading of information transferred to the audience through plot, dialogue, sets, and costumes. Conventional centres of interest and meaning were totally removed from the 'Happening'. The event was attended by the Queen's cousin, Lord Harewood, then Artistic Director of the Edinburgh Festival, and, importantly, was also televised on the BBC's *Monitor* programme. An unsuccessful case was later brought against the conference organisers in the Scottish Law Courts. The case was front page news for weeks in the UK and influenced the production of many similar events during the 1960s and 1970s (Haynes 1984: 61). A poetry conference proposed for the following year, however, was cancelled as a consequence of the furore. Meantime, the Traverse and Haynes himself had further identified themselves as *enfants terribles* in Scottish, and indeed wider British, cultural circles.

The 'Happening' in Edinburgh is a clear example of performance as ideological transaction. It generated a performance crisis by rupturing the accepted rules and norms which govern the use of signs and conventions in performance. A 'Happening' is seen from as many viewpoints as there are participants and witnesses. There is no common consent about its centres of interest or meaning. Its meaning is dynamically conditioned by contextuality and the spontaneous perceptions of those involved, who tend to respond to stimuli and incidents not specifically intended by the participants, stimuli and incidents often brought into meaning by reactions to prepared events thereby contributing to the potential for performance efficacy.

> The majority led by a harried Ken Tynan, apoplectic with rage, deplored the disturbance.... Celebrated directors from Yugoslavia, India, Ireland, and Germany called it 'nonsense' and 'child's play'. Joan Littlewood immediately sprang to its defence, dismissing questions such as 'What did it mean?', 'Was it Theatre?', 'Did it succeed?'Alexander Trocchi spat the word 'Dada' in Tynan's face and exclaimed that critics could not merely explain away new forces in art by bundling them into ready-made classifications. (Marowitz 1990: 62–63)

The press and some members of Edinburgh City Council expressed outrage. There were also many complaints about after hours drinking in the Traverse bar. At one point the Traverse came very close to losing its liquor licence in the spring of 1964. Thereafter it established a pattern of being open on Sundays and closed on Mondays. In the summer of 1965 the MP for Edinburgh West, Tory Anthony Stodart, expressed in the House of Commons his grave misgivings about the way in which public money was being spent at Edinburgh's Traverse Theatre Club to stage plays which would have been barred from performance in the ordinary theatres of the country on the grounds of obscenity or for other reasons.

In 1964 the Traverse produced a very successful production of *Happy End* by Weill and Brecht at Edinburgh University. At this time Calder was married to Bettina Jonic, the dancer, singer, and director, whose Croatian parents had brought her up in California. Jonic was a well-known interpreter of Brecht's work and had collaborated with Peter Brook and for a time later set up the Actors Work Group in London. Although not central to the argument of this book, she illustrates another example of the ways in which Americans and Europeans influenced alternative theatre in Britain and were themselves part of a mutual interaction between British and American theatre and culture generally at this time. The Calders and Haynes were listening to a recording of *Happy End* and decided to mount it at the Traverse, and *Happy End* was one of the hits of the 1964 Festival with Jonic performing. The production later went on to the Royal Court in London. Another Traverse production was Peter Weiss's *The Investigation* which was performed at the Unitarian Church in Edinburgh where Haynes had been married. It was directed by Michael Ockrent who was a young student at the time and later served as Director of the Traverse from May 1973 until November 1975 (Moffat 1978: 65).

Haynes edited *Traverse Plays* for Penguin (1966). He was already friends with Allen Lane who, as already noted, was an early supporter of the Paperback Bookshop following the controversy surrounding the selling of *Lady Chatterley's Lover*. A Heathcote Williams piece in the collection is entitled *The Local Stigmatic* (*Traverse Plays,* 1966). Harold Pinter had introduced Haynes to Williams's work. They became friends and later started the notorious magazine *SUCK* together in Amsterdam. Also in *Traverse Plays* were two Saul Bellow plays for which Marowitz got permission to produce at the Traverse. They were later done at the Fortune Theatre, London, then Off Broadway, then Broadway. Also included in *Traverse Plays* were Marguerite Duras's *La Musica* and *The Old Tune* by Robert Pinget adapted by Samuel Beckett. As this collection shows, the Traverse had the basic aim of putting on plays which the commercial theatre would not touch with the result that early on the theatre was constantly on the verge of financial crisis. The building itself was crumbling and was declared unsafe and had to be vacated in 1969. The theatre was able to survive the decade through subsidies from the Scottish Arts Council. Arts Council funding did not really pick up until after Haynes left although they did fund new writing with £100 and £200 grants. In 1966 the Arts Council subsidy was running at a rate of £7000 a year. Although the Traverse did not work with designers in the early days because of a perceived lack of funds, according to the website 'Measuring Worth', £7000 would amount to around a quarter of a million pounds in today's values. This can be seen as evidence of how innovative and valuable the work of the Traverse was seen to be by this time by the arts funding establishment. Even the Edinburgh City Council, then called the Edinburgh Corporation, contributed small sums of money. The Traverse did not make money in the way that some other contemporary arts groups did. A committee statement of January 1964 declared it not to be in the interests of members for the Traverse to become a cheap try-out theatre for commercial London managements. Nevertheless, it created an obvious line of profit whereby successful productions were sold on to other theatres often in London. Prestige and income were derived from transfers elsewhere.

Although it continues as an important and dynamic creative organisation, at first the Traverse established itself as a major 1960s institution which provided opportunities for new talent particularly among playwrights but also among actors, several of whom, including Tom Conti, subsequently became famous. Other key figures who were nurtured by the early Traverse include Lindsay Kemp and Jack Henry Moore, both of whom in turn made an early impact on the Traverse. Moore began life in Oklahoma. He gained a scholarship to the University of Oklahoma as an engineering student but then switched to a drama course and ended up working in New York, Off Broadway. On a trip to Boston with a friend he picked up a job in Dublin running a detective agency. During his time in Dublin he read an article about Haynes's production of *Happy End* and travelled to Edinburgh to meet Haynes. Haynes could not officially offer him a paid job because Moore did not have a work visa but Haynes offered him somewhere to stay and began to refer work to Moore unofficially (Haynes, 2009, UH).

Both Richard Demarco (2011) and Joyce McMillan (1988) claim that Moore was one of the main reasons why Haynes eventually left the Traverse. Moore was a very out gay man in Edinburgh when it was still not legal to be so and was also being paid under the table by Haynes to read and select scripts on behalf of himself and the Traverse. It was Moore who read and realised the importance of C.P. Taylor. Moore also spoke French and German and translated Brecht, Ionesco, and French playwrights. However, his unofficial role as Haynes's assistant created tension with members of the Traverse Committee.

It was when Haynes was staying with Moore in Dublin that he discovered Kemp was doing a show at the Dublin Theatre Festival. Kemp had used up his grant and was stranded and Haynes and

Moore helped raise money for Kemp to leave Dublin. Kemp went with them to Edinburgh and presented some of his early work there. He produced an adaptation of Dylan Thomas' *A Child's Christmas in Wales* and used Thomas's own recording of it in the production. Kemp performed in Genet plays during Festival time at a small space near the Traverse and claimed to be one of a long line of Great British mime artists, even claiming descent from Shakespeare's clown, Will Kemp. He later also worked at the Drury Lane Arts Lab and was a mentor to David Bowie who also performed at the Drury Lane Arts Lab.

Haynes was a consistently controversial figure and often completely at odds with other members of the committee. He had wanted to take Traverse productions to London for some time to extend their runs and investments. While he was still at the Traverse he produced a London season in 1965 at the Arts Theatre and lost money on it. He produced the season under the name of the London Traverse Theatre Company which did Tutte Lemkow's *Lecture to an Academy* (from Kafka). Marowitz directed Taylor's *Happy Days Are Here Again,* and *Green Julia* by Paul Ableman for LTTC. It was a critically successful season and Haynes began looking for a theatre to which he could use to send productions forward and back to Edinburgh.

Also in 1965 Haynes met Jennie Lee, then Minister for Arts, at a conference organised by the Arts Council in Colchester, called 'Problems of Small Theatre' at which he spoke. Lee encouraged him to try the Jeanetta Cochrane for the London Traverse and he did. He asked Ralph Koltai, Marowitz, and Michael Geliot to come and direct for him there. No state money was available, but Jennie Lee knew a West End producer named Frank Coven who put in £2,000 with a West End option on productions.

At the Annual General Meeting back in Edinburgh on 27 April 1966 Haynes declared that if members did not like his choice of plays, then he suggested they start their own theatre and he would join it. By the summer of 1966 Haynes's connection with the Traverse was effectively severed with Haynes himself living in London. He asked Nicholas Fairbairn, a prominent lawyer and supporter of the arts, and later an MP, to take over as Chair but, before his final break with Edinburgh, he enlisted the help of the influential figure, Arnold Goodman, and of Charles Marowitz in establishing the Traverse season at the Jeanetta Cochrane Theatre in London. After serving as both Artistic Director and Chairman of the Board for the Traverse, Jim Haynes resigned and settled in London on a full-time basis (Haynes 1984: 65). He was awarded the Whitbread prize for outstanding service to British theatre in May 1966.

In 1966 Marowitz and Haynes collaborated on the London Traverse season at the Jeanetta Cochrane Theatre. The Jeanetta Cochrane was leased to the Traverse for one year. Haynes did not like working there but two hits, already referred to, emerged from the season. Joe Orton's *Loot*, directed by Marowitz, transferred to the Piccadilly Theatre and won the Evening Standard Award for Best Production of 1966. The Bellow plays went to the Fortune Theatre and then New York.

In the years after Haynes's departure Max Stafford-Clark became the emblematic figure of the Traverse. Stafford-Clark was himself a theatre director who, as noted in a previous chapter, took a leave of absence from the Traverse in January 1968 to work with La MaMa in New York (McMillan 1988: 45). Previously, in February 1967 he had directed a triple-bill of plays by the La MaMa playwright Paul Foster at the Traverse under the umbrella title *Dead and Buried*. Then during May through August 1967 La MaMa toured performing Rochelle Owens's *Futz*, Paul Foster's *Tom Paine* and Sam Shepard's *Melodrama Play* in ten European cities, including the Edinburgh Festival. According to Stafford-Clark this period inspired the kind of theatrical experimentation seen in his subsequent work, represented in particular by the La MaMa (Stafford-Clark, 2009). Stafford-Clark followed O'Horgan's model in privileging workshop discovery over fixed text. It is important to note that his subsequent theatre practice also incorporated Stanislavski based research methodology.

> The difference was that Tom O'Horgan would not have thought of himself as a great text man. What he did was take a scenario and embellish it, transform it with the work he did with the music and so on. It always went beyond the word. The text was less important. The workshop to *engender* the text was something that came out of Joint Stock. That wasn't anything that La MaMa did. (Stafford-Clark 2007: 6)

Max Stafford-Clark left Trinity College, Dublin in 1966 and went straight to work at the Traverse Theatre. Early on he gained stage management experience at the Traverse and lived in West Bow and then Danube Street in a communal living situation. Originally he had been on a rugby tour with his university, Trinity College, Dublin, in Edinburgh and, rather than drinking with friends after matches (in which he was a good enough scrum-half to have been an international triallist for Ireland) had gone to the Traverse. There he met Richard Demarco and helped him to stuff envelopes on behalf of the theatre. Stafford-Clark, who had directed a review at Trinity, asked Jim Haynes if he could transfer it to the Traverse. They did it as a late night review called *Dublin Fair* and Stafford-Clark was invited back to do it at the Edinburgh Fringe Festival. They also received positive reviews and then transferred to London as part of the Traverse season at the Jeanette Cochrane Theatre (Stafford-Clark, 2009).

After returning from observing La MaMa in New York Stafford-Clark produced a paper at the Traverse in April 1968 which claimed that the most important single aspect of the Traverse was the encouragement and development of new playwrights. He argued that it was time for the Traverse to experiment in other directions as well. Stafford-Clark commented that the only director in Britain touching on these areas was Peter Brook of the Royal Shakespeare Company, as exemplified by *Marat/Sade* and *US*. Stafford-Clark worked with writers at the Traverse, including Megan Terry, Rochelle Owens, Howard Brenton, Stanley Eveling, and David Edgar, and dreamt at the time of having a permanent company and ensemble. But his aspirations were not to be fulfilled at the Traverse itself.

In November 1969 Stafford-Clark resigned as Director of the Traverse and formed the Traverse Workshop Company which maintained a link with the main Traverse organisation. Michael Rudman, an American Theatre Director, succeeded him as Director of the Traverse Theatre (1970–1973) and later became Artistic Director of the Hampstead Theatre (1973–1978) and Director of the Lyttelton Theatre at the National (1979–1982). The Traverse Workshop Company used the old Traverse space in James Court after the main Traverse organisation moved. Stafford-Clark's Company lived and rehearsed there in the way of a hippie commune. The seeds of Stafford-Clark works were sown during the 1960s (Stafford-Clark, 2009) and subsequently developed further with Joint Stock, the Royal Court, and Out of Joint.

International Times

Haynes started the newspaper *International Times* on the 14th October 1966 at The Roundhouse in Chalk Farm, London. Haynes started the *International Times* with Moore, John Hopkins, Jeff Nuttall and Barry Miles. Lord Goodman, previously a supporter, cooled towards him as he thought the paper supported drug taking, which it did not, though it tried to take the hysteria out of the debate. Haynes started the paper because he realised how much money the Cochrane was wasting on advertising and thought, if the group had its own paper, it would save on promotion costs, which he claims it did. The *IT* was an immediate success, with good sales and an avid readership. It became a mouthpiece for the London Underground scene. Haynes himself was one of the first street sellers pitching copies, as mentioned in an earlier chapter, outside of the Aldwych Theatre when Peter Brook's *US* played there. *IT* was important in spreading the word about alternative productions going on at the time. The cost for a copy was one shilling. Haynes borrowed £125 (£1,910 today according to the website Measuring Worth) to pay the printers to do the first issue. For a time the paper was run from the basement of Miles's bookshop Indica on Southampton Row. Lots of writing was also done at Haynes's house.

Haynes tried to present underground films and 'Happenings' at the Cochrane but the management was not keen on it. There were lunchtime theatre productions and talks, including an event with Saul Bellow, but Haynes claims he was very frustrated. The productions were costly and therefore had to be successful at the Box Office. Haynes was ready to throw in the towel and set about trying to find a space in Covent Garden. In 1967 he found a couple of empty warehouses at the top of Drury Lane (no. 184) and persuaded the owner to let him have them as an arts space until he required them for commercial use. A three-month notice was to be given. Haynes lived in Drury Lane at the back of the Arts Lab and in Long Acre over a fruit and vegetable shop. His place in Long Acre had a pay phone and people used to drop by for a cup of tea and to use the phone. Haynes had been given a pre-release copy of *Sergeant Pepper* by the Beatles and people also dropped by to listen to that. The apartment had four rooms. Haynes and Jack Henry Moore lived there with many others coming and going.

Haynes met the Beatles through Brian Epstein who asked to meet him. Haynes was friendly with John Lennon and Miles got close to Paul McCartney. The Beatles gave some money to fund the

IT. Haynes claims he knew Yoko Ono before she met John Lennon. When Yoko Ono came over from New York she organised one of her first 'Happenings' at the Cochrane. The launch party for the *IT* was held at the Roundhouse. Arnold Wesker let Haynes have the keys while he was trying to get Centre 42 up and running. 5,000 people attended and Pink Floyd and Soft Machine performed. Paul McCartney and Monica Vitti also attended. The *IT* became an underground newspaper and an alternative to mainstream media.

> A new radicalism was in the air: the launching of Britain's first underground newspaper (*International Times*) marks the point at which the counter-culture acquired a recognisable voice. (Hewison 1986: 94)

The *International Times* quickly became concerned with the preoccupations of the protest movement as well as with sex and drugs rather than political revolution strictly speaking.

Time Out

While still an undergraduate, Tony Elliot started assisting Jim Haynes at the *International Times*. In 1968 Elliot founded his own publication *Time Out* as an alternative to *What's On in London* with, according to Jim Haynes, Haynes's help and encouragement. According to his own report, Haynes provided guidance and helped to produce the first copies of *Time Out* which Haynes then handed out together with the *International Times* in front of the Aldwych Theatre while Peter Brook's production of *US* was performing (Haynes, 2011, DWIC).

In 1968 the magazine added the 'Fringe' category to the theatre section, borrowing the term from the Edinburgh Festival Fringe (Haynes 1984: 151–152). The categories established by *Time Out* in its theatre listings were writer's theatre, experimental theatre, performance art, political theatre, and community theatre. This new categorisation in *Time Out* became important in shaping the scope of the alternative theatre scene and even how groups later defined themselves. It is this chronology of events which marks the transmission of the kind of work originally seen during the Edinburgh Fringe Festival to London and more widely to the rest of Britain. Today there are also Fringe Festivals in Toronto, New York, and Hollywood, California.

Jeff Nuttall (1933–2004), who was an original staff contributor to the *International Times* from its founding in 1966, also co-founded the People Show with his neighbour Mark Long in 1966. Nuttall wrote and acted with the People Show for five years including the period when it was based at the Drury Lane Arts Lab (Anon, *Guardian*, 2004). The People Show was—and was intended to be—an important catalyst in the performance art movement and incorporated American arts forms such as 'Happenings', Jazz, and oral verse inspired by members of the Beat generation of poets such as William Burroughs. Nuttall detailed an important generational shift in *Bomb Culture* (1968), a manifesto intended to capture the spirit of the post-Hiroshima generation which came of age after World War II and was burdened with the existential threat posed by the cold war. *Bomb Culture* was also a chronicle of the emerging counterculture in Britain (Miles 2010: 235).

1967 and the founding of the Drury Lane Arts Lab

As noted earlier, after highly successful engagements organised in collaboration with the Traverse Theatre, the La MaMa Troupe directed by Tom O'Horgan performed *Futz* at the Mercury Theatre in Notting Hill and then *Tom Paine* at the Vaudeville Theatre in London's West End. The Open Theatre directed by Joseph Chaikin performed *America Hurrah* at the Royal Court. The summer of 1967 would later be referred to as the 'American Summer' (Ansorge 1975: 22). As John Arden stated at the time:

> What they have managed to do with both *Futz* and *Tom Paine* is to arouse a quite remarkable degree of excitement among informed and receptive theatre workers in the city. La MaMa Troupe's visit here is going to have a very great effect upon the work done in England over the next few years. I know my own writing is already being influenced considerably. (Bottoms 2004: 202)

Following the work of American experimental companies in London during the summer of 1967 Haynes, as noted previously, started the Arts Lab during August 1967 in a warehouse at the top of Drury Lane. It ran from Drury Lane at the front to facing the City Lit building at the back with three floors. The warehouse was converted into a variety of spaces for art exhibitions, theatre performances, music, and cinema. This multi-media laboratory and centre of fertilisation only lasted for fifteen months but in that time introduced a new generation of writers, directors, and actors who would go on to produce work of national and international significance. Important groups emerging from the Drury Lane Arts Lab onto the British theatrical landscape included Freehold, Portable Theatre, Pip Simmons Group, London La MaMa, and the People Show. Nonetheless, Lord Goodman, then Chairman of the Arts Council, would not allow the Arts Council to support the Drury Lane Arts Lab because of its perceived drug culture.

As soon as the People Show got the keys to the Drury Lane Arts Lab building, and before anything else was done to it, they presented a production with cages. (They also did future productions at the Drury Lane Arts Lab.) The main building was a gallery. The cinema in the basement had no seats, just foam rubber to sit on. The first floor housed the restaurant and was also used for site-specific work. The back included dressing rooms and was also where Haynes lived. People lived and stayed in different spaces. Without any announcement the Drury Lane Arts Lab opened, and through word of mouth became a popular success with people coming from all over Europe to see it. Haynes sent duplicate letters out to those included in *Who's Who in Theatre* and key figures in cinema asking them to be Patrons for £50 a year. Membership was £2 or £5 and for students £1. £30,000 was raised that way and Peter Brook and Tom Stoppard were Patrons. The current equivalent of this amount would be approximately between £446,800 and £872,100, depending on the inflator used. This demonstrates that, as in Scotland, Haynes was able to raise considerable amounts of money in England, despite his reputation as an anti-establishment rebel.

Jack Henry Moore ran the theatre in Drury Lane and lived there. David Curtis ran the cinema and his wife Biddy Pippin, with Pamela Zoline, ran the gallery. Steven Berkoff became involved in the Drury Lane Arts Lab early on and asked Haynes to let him have a space where he then produced his first show, *Metamorphosis* by Kafka. Tuesday night was an open night when the Arts Lab would show work that people brought in. There were lots of French films and New York underground films. People came from all over the world to see what the Arts Lab was up to.

John Lennon and Yoko Ono had an exhibition in the gallery in August 1968 as a German television crew interviewed Haynes about the Drury Lane Arts Lab. The film crew asked to interview them too. After the German broadcast, hundreds of backpackers started coming over from Germany to experience the Drury Lane Arts Lab. This began a change of audience at the Arts Lab. When the Arts Lab started, the average audience age of its audience was around thirty, although mixed. There after audiences became much younger and the Arts Lab began to feel like a youth club. This had the effect of keeping away a mixture of ages and a greater cross-section of the public (Haynes, 2011, DWIC).

A pervasive anti-Vietnam War sentiment at the time was expressed through plays, demonstrations, and articles. People on the run asked to be hidden (Haynes, 2009, UH). Many potential draftees were illegally in Britain. You could stay in Britain for three months on a US passport and many people just did not leave. Jack Henry Moore, for example, was never living legally in Britain. He spoke Dutch, German, and French and was for many years a consultant to U.N.E.S.C.O. holding a U.N.E.S.C.O. passport. Moore received financial support from the Dutch government for a project called 'Bank' which was a video library. Someone then reported him to the tax authorities and the project was shut down (Haynes 2009, UH).

Perhaps the most important single production at the Drury Lane Arts Lab was *Vagina Rex and the Gas Oven* in 1969 by the writer, director, and actor Jane Arden. The production employed multimedia effects and used surreal and mystical montage in exploring a woman's attempt to come to terms with the sense of inferiority imposed on her by a patriarchal society. A substantial number of people came together for it, including Jane Arden, Jack Bond, Sheila Allen, and Victor Spinetti who already knew each other. There was an enthusiastic response from the underground audiences and glitterati and when it finished at the Drury Lane Arts Lab, Marowitz offered it a home at the Open Space but it never moved. Haynes feels that Jack Bond and Jane Arden wanted a higher profile venue (Haynes, 2009, UH). John Calder then published *Vagina Rex and the Gas Oven*.

The people who actually ran the Drury Lane Arts Lab lived there or nearby. There were no formal meetings and initially the publicity was mainly through the *International Times*. Then other papers picked up on Arts Lab activities and publicity spread by word of mouth. The cinema only held sixty to eighty people and the theatre audience capacity depended on the particular configuration. Padded beer crates were kept outside and when people bought their tickets they carried their seats in with them. Tickets were very cheap and often if people could not pay they were passed in for free. The rich and famous on the other hand were expected to pay. The restaurant took in money but there was no alcohol licence.

There was an empty hotel a few doors down from the Drury Lane Arts Lab which Lab participants seized and housed with homeless people. Eventually the police poured cement into the drains and it was possibly the first squatters' seizure in London. At the weekends people who came from outside of London would stay in the cinema and gallery overnight. The actors in *Hair* auditioned and rehearsed at the Drury Lane Arts Lab. The Drury Lane Arts Lab could quite justly represent itself as the focal point of the underground. As already noted, it failed to get the endorsement of Arts Council Chairman Arnold Goodman but it did have the informal support of the government Arts Minister Jenny Lee.

Many commentators identify the Drury Lane Arts Lab as the very birthplace of the alternative theatre movement in Britain (Ansorge 1975, Itzin 1980, Kershaw 1992,) and by 1977 there were over 170 community-based, multi-media Arts Labs scattered throughout the UK. While other Arts Labs started up in Birmingham, Manchester, and elsewhere, Nicholas Albery created *The Arts Labs News* which gave an update on the arts labs' activities every two or three months. The proliferation of activity at the Arts Lab was a direct result of Haynes's policies. The Drury Lane Arts Lab did not practice artistic vetting and for this reason provided a free space for young artists and groups of artists such as Freehold and Pip Simmons to experiment and develop their respective voices. The Edinburgh Festival Fringe had pioneered this practice, since its foundation in 1947, and so may have influenced Haynes's approach by example. Further the Drury Lane Arts Lab quickly became one of the most influential multi-media centres in the entire world. Many television stations throughout Europe and Japan made programmes about the Drury Lane Arts Lab (Haynes 1984: 151). The Drury Lane Arts Lab created a timetabled space to try new things out free from the commercial constraints of having to please an audience. It also encouraged widespread participation and facilitated participatory performance practices which became a characteristic of the alternative theatre in Britain (Haynes 1984:151).

It is important to note how the 'gathering phase' and 'dispersal phase' as defined by Kershaw (Kershaw 1992) were organised differently for the audience than in a traditional British theatre. The Drury Lane Arts Lab had a deliberately informal atmosphere and was a meeting place for many. The various spaces within the Drury Lane Arts Lab were constantly changing, dependent on the showing currently offered. Whatever happened to be showing during any given day or evening was displayed on a blackboard near the front entrance. The audience was not seated in a conventional manner but sat on mats or crates placed on the floor. All of these factors contributed to a collapse of traditional hierarchies within the activities at the Drury Lane Arts Lab. In this way the Drury Lane Arts Lab facilitated efficacious radical performance and ideological transaction which may reasonably be presumed to have brought about essential changes in the audiences' perceptions. This in turn may have had an impact on the spectators' future relationship with society; in any case it had an immediate effect on their cultural experience.

Haynes ran the Drury Lane Arts Lab from 1967 to 1969 but at the end there were problems with police raids because of the drug-taking on the premises and because Haynes had also started the controversial magazine *SUCK*. There was also a lack of financial control and the money that Haynes raised had been spent.

It is ironic, then, that the venue which has often been credited as the birthplace of the alternative theatre was very short-lived. The American expatriate Jim Haynes opened the Drury Lane Arts Lab in 1968, and it has now achieved legendary status as a kind of creative crucible for its times (Kershaw 1992: 100).

1968–1969

Haynes's activities at this time were somewhat scattergun in their approach. He engaged multiple performance spaces. In 1968 Haynes hired the Albert Hall for a fundraiser, originally to star Leonard Cohen. He could not attend but John Lennon, Yoko Ono and others did. Someone in the audience began to strip. When the officials tried to remove her, others joined in. It was later called *The Alchemical Wedding*. A second venue was the UFO Space in Charing Cross Road. UFO Space was an Irish drinking club and one night a week it was dark. Haynes persuaded UFO's owners to let him hire it for that one night. UFO Space became *the* London underground meeting place. Pink Floyd and Soft Machine were launched there. There were market stalls, poster shops and an *IT* stand. UFO Space ran smoothly until the *News of the World* published a negative article on it. Haynes also had a third performance space. He got the key from the estate agents to a property underneath the corner of Tottenham Court Road, Charing Cross Road, and Oxford Street. He hosted late night parties with bands in an enormous space that was bigger than the Roundhouse. The Living Theatre did an event there and Dick Gregory, the African-American comic, did an event for 300 to 400 people. Dick Gregory was then also a Presidential candidate and Haynes was his Europe campaign manager.

After the Drury Lane Arts Lab closed Haynes moved between Paris and Amsterdam. He set up the sexual freedom newspaper *SUCK* and directed the White Dream Film Festival in Amsterdam. He believed that sexual images by definition were not obscene. For him, obscenity is hunger, no shelter, and violence, but not sexual imagery. In his view, if such imagery brings pleasure to the people involved it amounts to a social contract and others cannot contest this. That was the point he says he was trying to make (Haynes, 2009, UH). Haynes finds pornography boring but erotica stimulating and exciting. It was his idea to start *SUCK*, recruiting

Germaine Greer, Heathcote Williams, Bill Levy, Sarah Jensen, Susanne Brögger, and Lynn Tillman as contributors. Germaine Greer was a jury member at the White Dream Film Festival. About a dozen issues of *SUCK* were published, as well as a book, and additional festivals also took place. All of them made an impact at the time and led Haynes at one point to have tea with Salvador Dali.

Haynes went to live in Paris in late 1969, while at the same time, he started *SUCK* in Amsterdam. He had developed a relationship with certain Parisian professors who brought groups of students over to both the Traverse and then the Drury Lane Arts Lab. He received an invitation to be a visiting professor at a new experimental University in Paris, the University at Vincennes (Paris 8), later relocated to St Denis, teaching sexual politics. Haynes said he could not speak French and they said he could teach in English. He taught at Vincennes for thirty years as a founding staff member.

Conclusion

It is important to put Jim Haynes's enormous impact in context. In Edinburgh, for example, individual initiatives had turned the general artistic legacy of World War II into something important to many. The Edinburgh International Festival of Music and the Arts was launched in 1947. In the same year, around the mainstream festival venues, a 'fringe' emerged involving eight theatre groups which performed for three weeks during the summer festival. This movement, which was first referred to as the Fringe in 1948, started as a protest because Unity Theatre had been excluded from the 'main' festival. A coordinating body called the Fringe Society was founded immediately after the festival in 1958 and was fully in operation for the festival of 1959.

Edinburgh already had a long established literary culture which was mainly focused around certain pubs. Edinburgh University enrolled a cosmopolitan student population and there was a then independent and innovative Art College. Eventually, though, there was a longing for a permanent home in which the excitement and experimental work of the Festival could be prolonged throughout the year. This was the basis on which the Traverse Theatre and Gallery were founded. Haynes may have been in the right place at the right time, but his talent and influence ensured that his legacy would reach far, wide, and deep. That this was quickly recognised can be seen in Harold Hobson's words when Haynes announced that he would leave the Traverse:

> I cannot think of any happier preliminary to the 1966 Festival than that Mr Haynes should be asked to reconsider his resignation. It is, I repeat, a matter of international importance in the theatre. (Moffat 1978: 60)

The Traverse Theatre itself was one of the most important sub-cultural developments of its time. Without Jim Haynes it would almost certainly never have achieved the role or importance it developed. Haynes's influence, as we have seen, reached far wider audiences after he left the Traverse. Many of those he influenced and supported remain key contributors to alternative British theatre.

As mentioned previously many identify the Drury Lane Arts Lab as the very birthplace of the alternative theatre movement in Britain. This book does not agree with such an absolute assertion, but argues that the significance of the Drury Lane Arts Lab is hard to overstate. The Drury Lane Arts Lab was similar to the Traverse in that Haynes brought together in it a wide variety of activities including theatre, music, poetry, and visual art. Perhaps most importantly, the Drury Lane Arts Lab was a space which created an intersection between ideas and creative individuals. In bringing these elements together Haynes created a seedbed for the germination of new personal associations, collaborations, and new forms of creative output. If performance is being considered in cultural, social, and political spheres, there is no doubt the Arts Lab was highly efficacious. In pursuing the theme of such efficacy, we now turn our attention to Haynes's close friend and collaborator, Charles Marowitz.

Chapter Five: Charles Marowitz

This chapter considers the impact and influence of Charles Marowitz's theatre practice on alternative theatre in Britain during his London period 1956–1980. Specifically, the chapter looks at Marowitz's influence on the establishment of the London Fringe and in expanding the parameters of alternative theatre engagement with British society during this time period. Marowitz reinvigorated the classics by rigorously bending and stretching masterpieces in the form of free adaptations and collages. Furthermore, this chapter considers certain controversies associated with Marowitz which impacted on the parameters of censorship in Britain both before and after the Theatres Act of 1968. This portion of the book seeks to analyse and discuss these developments within the broader context of American influence on alternative British Theatre 1956–1980.

During the early 1950s Marowitz considered American life to be dominated by superficiality and conformity. He was drafted by the US Army during the Korean War but ended up spending two years stationed in France. He believed French culture could have a civilising influence upon him and began to imagine that he would have a more meaningful life in Europe. In due course he endeavoured to find a drama academy in France that he would be able to attend. However, there were no G.I. Bill approved drama schools in France whereas in England there were approved drama schools in both Glasgow and London. Marowitz opted to train at the London Academy of Music and Dramatic Art in the hope that he would be able to return to France on a regular basis.

The life and career of the late Charles Marowitz (1932–2014) of course did not occur in isolation but within a complex fabric of associations with a wide range of individuals, institutions, and communities. During his London period from 1956 to 1980 Marowitz's theatre practice and criticism were influential in injecting radical creativity into the British theatre. Marowitz's work revolved around utilising aesthetic and intellectual tools to upset the status quo. Marowitz agitated conventional British theatre at the time by reinvigorating the classics, writing irreverent theatre criticism, and fulfilling the inherent nature of alternative theatre in helping to establish what might be seen a dialectical relationship between the alternative sector and the commercial theatre establishment. This abrasion had the effect of shaking things loose, calling various received notions into question, and generally turning accepted conventions on their head. For better or for worse Marowitz's abrasion also expressed itself in his personality and affected his working relationships with various collaborators. Through analysis of a series of key events, theatrical influences, and personal associations a cumulative portrait of Charles Marowitz's contribution to British alternative theatre will emerge.

During the earlier period of his career Marowitz was caught up in prevailing theatrical preoccupations of the day. During the 1960s his theatrical temperament transformed from an interest in applying Stanislavski's methodology to the ideas of Artaud whom he first read in 1958. In his own sensibility Marowitz shifted away from socially committed plays and ideology to an emphasis on aesthetic innovation and metaphysical exploration. In particular, when he was working with the Traverse he found that there was a predominant emphasis on new writing. He decided that no amount of new writing would really change theatre itself or free it from a state of aesthetic obsolescence so he began to search for new forms and techniques which would transcend the mundane and the temporal (Marowitz 1973: 8–9). He became committed to the creation of a collective instrument based around the idea of a permanent company. Working collectively in collaboration with a director but without specific reference to a single playwright *per se* would, in his view, by virtue of its artistic chemistry, create a new and original kind of artistic specimen that was more efficacious than the written word itself (Marowitz, Interview, 2011). It was in order to realise this vision that Marowitz originally collaborated with Peter Brook on the Theatre of Cruelty season in 1963/64, which effectively popularised the ideas of Artaud within British theatre. He later created the Open Space Theatre Company in 1968 which was the only example in Britain of a laboratory company run on a repertory basis. Marowitz's development in this direction started with his experience of the Group Theatre and the emergence of the 'American Method' or rather American derivations of Stanislavski. In particular, Stanislavski-based improvisational techniques were an important formative influence on Marowitz.

Early Years

Marowitz was raised in poverty, the third child of exclusively Yiddish-speaking Polish immigrants, on the Lower East Side of New York City and at the age of sixteen read *The Fervent Years* (1945) by Harold Clurman. Clurman detailed the troubled history of the Group Theatre (1931–1941). At the age of seventeen Marowitz founded his own acting company on the Lower East Side of New York. In 1950, while still in High School Marowitz became the youngest theatre critic for the newly formed *Village Voice* and experienced first-hand the advent of the Off Broadway movement. Greenwich Village, where Marowitz spent his youth, was also the site of Off Broadway Theatres. 'Off Broadway' was a geographical demarcation but also had roots in definitions of the alternative theatre movement in America (Aronson 2000). Later, after his move to London and the end of his studies at the London Academy of Music and Dramatic Art in 1957, and the Central School of Speech and

Drama in 1958, he began to teach a workshop for British actors based on the principles and practices of the American Method.

London

At the age of twenty-four Charles Marowitz moved to London, during the summer of 1956. Continental influences as well as new American drama were beginning to open new possibilities for the future direction of the British Theatre (Shellard 1999: 17). Along with the work of Ionesco and Adamov and the London premiere of *Waiting for Godot* in 1955 at the Arts Theatre, Joan Littlewood's productions of Brecht promised change in theatre subject matter and practices. These productions were followed by the London tour of the Berliner Ensemble in the autumn of 1956. On 8 May 1956, *Look Back in Anger* premiered at the Royal Court Theatre. Though the fact is not discussed nearly as much, the previous month, April 1956, also saw the Royal Court produce the London premiere of Arthur Miller's *The Crucible.*

The Suez crisis as well as the Hungarian uprising in 1956 led to reverberations in British society including the emergence of the 'New Left' which was later to have an impact on politically inclined alternative theatre and performance (Itzin 1980). Other factors such as the growing power of young people, changes in family relationships, and new standards of sexual behavior would lead to widespread social upheaval in the two decades which followed. As a relative outsider Marowitz became conscious of certain tendencies within British culture. He found people obsessed with class identity. He found a society in the midst of radical change, given to dissent, anti-establishment fervor, and new trends which were convulsing British culture. He also found American influence to be pervasive in such areas as music and cinema. Later on, the Vietnam protest movement and drug use among the younger generation (Marowitz 1990: 2–3) were further indicators he witnessed.

According to Marowitz, he became aware at LAMDA for the first time of the British as opposed to the American approach to acting. He developed a perception that the British approach was somewhat weighted towards voice and movement. He found that from his point of view, the British approach at the time was almost exclusively concerned with externals and uninterested in the concept of inner technique (Rebellato 1999: 78). In his view, Stanislavsky was given mindless lip service. Only one class at LAMDA theoretically touched on his ideas, a bi-weekly improvisation session. Marowitz considered these sessions to be a travesty of Method work, consisting exclusively of improvisations of little playlets worked up by the students under the instructor's supervision. When some of the other American students who were already versed in the Method suggested that the work they were doing was devoid of appropriate actions, subtext, and palpable contact, the instructor did not appear to understand or be versed in the terminology they were using (Marowitz 1990: 14–15). Marowitz became bitterly disillusioned at LAMDA as did two of his American classmates who left the course. Marowitz wanted to follow suit but had he done so he would have lost his G.I. Bill subsidy and would have had to return to the United States, which he was unwilling to do.

Marowitz considered the training at LAMDA to be backward, although he did encounter some interesting work on verse technique and he was exposed to the habits of established British classical theatre practitioners. He found that acting was thought to be merely a mode of projecting language and physical technique. In his view the school was—intellectually and artistically—a kind of British feeder for the West End theatre establishment and he felt himself becoming increasingly anti-social. Marowitz decided to branch out into the London theatre itself and directed his first theatre production in Britain at the London Unity Theatre. He directed a production of his own adaptation of Gogol's comedy *Marriage* and the production received a favourable notice in *The Times* (Marowitz 1990: 17). Marowitz was then asked to work on a Living Newspaper called *World on Edge* being devised at Unity in November 1956 on the subject of the recent Suez crisis and the Hungarian uprising (Chambers 1989: 340–345).

Shortly after that production Marowitz started a Method workshop at Unity Theatre which he used to introduce a number of English actors to the principles and ideas of Stanislavsky although Unity had run a Stanislavsky based school in the late 1930s (Chambers 1989: 361). He also developed his own exercises and ideas. Marowitz decided that instead of using material such as Clifford Odets, Gorky, and Arthur Miller he would use Shakespeare, Marlowe, and Webster (Marowitz 1990: 17). After one year at LAMDA Marowitz transferred to the Central School of Speech and Drama but found his experience there to be very similar to that at LAMDA and after his G.I. Bill subsidy ran out, the Method workshop became his primary source of income. He immersed himself as much as possible in the study and practice of Stanislavsky but found that applying this practice to texts by Shakespeare, Marlowe, and Webster was problematic just as others such as Michel St Denis had found before him. Marowitz soon became associated with the Method label and at the age of twenty-nine, wrote his first book entitled *The Method as Means* (1961).

In-Stage

Marowitz read Artaud for the first time during 1958 and also began writing criticism for the *Encore Reader* magazine, the theatrical bi-monthly publication, which was originally started by Clive Goodwin in 1954 (Marowitz, Milne, Hale eds. 1965). Also in 1958 Marowitz persuaded the British Drama League to allow him to convert a rooftop studio at Fitzroy Square in London into his own experimental theatre which he then called 'In-Stage' (Miles 2010: 125).

At In-Stage Marowitz attempted to define a non-naturalistic style, building on the theories of the early Absurdist and Surrealists. This effort involved essentially a paring down of language as far as possible while establishing an ingrained awareness of what things are essentially, rather than what they seem to be on the surface. Marowitz's experimental work was intended to run in parallel with classical theatre productions and commercial theatre, and was warmly received by the critic Alan Pryce-Jones of *The Observer* (Marowitz 1990: 19–20). In-Stage went on to produce a play by J.B. Lynne called *The Trigon* with performances by Timothy West and Prunella Scales. *The Trigon* transferred to Brighton and then the Arts Theatre Club. At In-Stage Marowitz also mounted the British premiere of Samuel Beckett's *Act Without Words II*, Arthur Miller's *The Man Who Had All the Luck*, and William Saroyan's *The Cave Dwellers*. In-Stage was also the first theatre in Britain to produce works by the playwright Murray Schisgal. This was the period immediately before Marowitz's affinity for Artaud found expression in his theatre practice.

> Before long—one can never date these things but it was around the early Sixties—I realized I had been blinded by Strasberg in precisely the same way he had been conned by Stanislavski, and that in some kind of prophetic way, my attempt to apply Method to classics was really an indication of an entirely different temperament, one which found its realisation in the ideas of Artaud. (Hewison 1986: 90–91)

At the In-Stage theatre at Fitzroy Square spectators would line up in a small room below the rooftop studio where they were offered tea and biscuits by Marowitz's friend and collaborator Gillian Watt. When the show was about to start audience members would move in single file up the narrow staircase that led to the tiny platform stage. Marowitz would often be backstage working the lights and sound tape. After the performance the audience would file out and Gillian Watt would stand at the bottom of the staircase holding a wicker basket into which members of the audience would drop coins and sometimes notes. At In-Stage the actors received no wages and the audience paid no admission, which was also a characteristic of many contemporaneous Off Off Broadway theatres in New York (Crespy 2003). The productions were both offbeat and highbrow as were the audiences. Many of the audience members were readers of *The New Statesman* which, along with the British Drama League magazine, were the only publications In-Stage could afford to advertise in. The audiences at In-Stage formed the beginnings of a new theatre-going public, a public which would eventually patronise places such as the Roundhouse, UFO, Ambiance, Soho Poly, the Oval House, and the Open Space. These were the forerunners of what would eventually become the London Fringe.

Theatre of Cruelty

When Marowitz arrived in London in 1956 he was still writing and reviewing regularly for *The Village Voice* which first coined the term 'Off Off Broadway' in 1960. As discussed, once in London Marowitz started writing for *The Encore Reader* as well. In fact *The Encore Reader* was what originally brought Peter Brook and Charles Marowitz together as they were both regular contributors (Marowitz 1990: 81). One of the first productions Marowitz had seen after moving to Britain was Peter Brook's 1957 production of *Titus Andronicus* at Stratford-upon-Avon, which Marowitz reviewed for the *Village Voice*. In the review Marowitz stated, 'A short scalene-shaped man named Peter Brook, aged 33, is the greatest director in England' (Marowitz 1990: 81). One of the things which had attracted Marowitz to the *Encore* publication was its association with Brook. Marowitz wrote a letter to Brook and invited him to a production he was directing at In-Stage of *A Little Something for the Maid* by Ray Abell and Brook attended. Afterwards Brook and

Marowitz met in London and then again in Paris where Brook originally introduced Marowitz to the idea of collaborating on the 1962 production of *King Lear* with Paul Scofield and then later on an experimental season with the Royal Shakespeare Company.

Together Brook and Marowitz were primarily responsible for the injection of Artaud's ideas into contemporary theatre practice (Kershaw 1992: 103). During 1963/64 Charles Marowitz and Peter Brook put Artaud's ideas to the test with the Royal Shakespeare Company Experimental Group/Theatre of Cruelty at LAMDA. Initially Brook brought Marowitz into the RSC as his assistant on the famous 1962 production of *King Lear* and it was through that relationship that the Theatre of Cruelty group came about (Chambers 2004: 152). The group's stated intention was 'to explore certain problems of acting and stagecraft in laboratory conditions, without the commercial pressures of public performance' (Cole and Chinoy 1970: 430). This was the first full-fledged experimental project of its kind in Britain. Artaud saw the conventional use of language in theatre as a means of repressing society (Sontag in Artaud 1988: np). Artaud's emphasis on non-verbal communication through movement and sound has influenced a trend in contemporary British theatre towards prioritising the body over conventional literary interpretation.

It was Marowitz's job during the first three months of the *Theatre of Cruelty* project to devise a series of exercises by which the actors' untapped creativity could be accessed (Burns 1972: 178–179). This involved an effort to engage with areas of the actors' minds and bodies which lay beneath, inaccessible to the conventional naturalistic techniques on which contemporary actors predominantly based their performances. Marowitz believed that Stanislavsky's most important discovery was the notion of 'subtext'. Behind surface existence was something resembling a complex of needs, drives, symbols, and unformulated emotions which existed in the realm Artaud described as 'that fragile fluctuating centre which forms never reach' (Marowitz 1990: 85–86). The exercises Marowitz invented were intended to penetrate the realm of the actors' primitive drives. They were designed to coax the actor into sounds, movements, spatial metaphors, and non-verbal improvisations which potentially derived from a place where individual human communication originates.

During the period when the *Theatre of Cruelty* was being formed it was also Marowitz's job to audition actors who might join the experimental company (as distinct from the main RSC). Marowitz looked for actors who were open enough to accommodate highly unorthodox techniques. Instead of seeing actors on a one-to-one basis, Marowitz worked out a system of collective auditions whereby groups of eight and ten would interact with one another through improvisations, nonsense texts, and various theatre games engineered to test both their imaginations and their critical temperament. One of the actors who auditioned was then an unknown actor named Glenda Jackson. After her work with the RSC Experimental Group Jackson went on to become a prominent star of stage and screen, receiving two Academy Awards for Best Actress before she turned to politics, serving as a long-time Labour MP, representing Hampstead and Highgate in north London.

Unlike a traditional rehearsal process which begins after actors have already been cast in particular roles, the Theatre of Cruelty's creative process involved Marowitz and Brook putting the actors through a series of tests and exercises which primarily included improvisations and games in which actors' personal imaginations were constantly being provoked into outward expression. The showing of the company's work was a kind of surrealist vaudeville selection (Hewison 1986: 91). Pieces explored psychic interiors and the extremes of performance with wild bouts of violence and cruelty (Davies 1987: 159) while incorporating a variety of authors' work (including John Arden, Shakespeare, Paul Ableman, Alain Robbe-Grillet, and others).

It was also during this season that Marowitz first wrote and directed his twenty-eight minute version of the collage *Hamlet* which was later expanded to eighty minutes. Marowitz's eighty-minute version of his collage *Hamlet* was first produced with In-Stage for the Literarisches Colloquium, Berlin, at the Akademie der Kunste in 1965. It went on to the Jeanetta Cochrane Theatre in London in 1966 (Schiele 2005: 3). The company also presented a version of Genet's *The Screens* at the Donmar Studio, established in 1961 by West End producer Donald Albery as a rehearsal space for his production company Donmar Productions (whose name is derived from the first three letters of his name and his wife's middle name, Margaret) and the RSC then turned the space into a theatre called The Warehouse (Chambers 2004: 72). Later, the company of eighteen actors was integrated into the main Royal Shakespeare Company and went on to utilise the language and techniques developed during the Theatre of Cruelty for the 1964 production of Peter Weiss's *Marat/Sade,* directed by Peter Brook. Marowitz was offered a permanent position with the company but he turned it down because he did not want to become trapped in Brook's shadow.

Controversy in Glasgow

On opening night in December 1965, the Board of the Glasgow Citizens Theatre cancelled a production of Marlowe's *Dr. Faustus* to be held in its studio, the Close Theatre, and directed by Marowitz, with a full audience in attendance. Marowitz had put together a new adaptation drawing a parallel between Dr. Faustus and J. Robert Oppenheimer. His version was intended to provide insight into Faustus who experiments with forbidden knowledge and Oppenheimer, the scientist who arguably transgressed against the permissible bounds of human endeavour in being primarily responsible for the creation of the atomic bomb. Such had been the impetus for previous productions such as Theatre Workshop's *Uranium 235* and the *Life of Galileo* by Bertolt Brecht. Faustus was dressed lLife ike a modern university science research scholar and sat at a desk with modern lab equipment. Mephistopheles was portrayed as a government defense chief who appropriates scientists for the purpose of obtaining military dominance.

Since the adaptation had been given a modern setting Marowitz felt that the Seven Deadly Sins needed to be appropriately reinterpreted. Marowitz decided to identify each of the Seven Deadly Sins with a caricature mask of a different modern head of state. For Sloth he chose a mask of Queen Elizabeth II. At the final preview the chairman of the management committee at the theatre in which the production was to open objected to the caricature on the grounds that it was in bad taste and would be offensive to members of a Scottish audience. He insisted that the Queen was not slothful and in fact worked very hard on state occasions, on diplomatic visits, and at local and regional events. Marowitz pointed out that the work was not in fact personal to the Queen but that she herself was symbolic of a certain class in British society which many perceived as slothful, living on inherited incomes, lounging around in huge mansions, and holding aristocratic titles.

The next day the chairman of the management committee as well as other members of the theatre's board confronted Marowitz and asked him if he would delete the impersonation of the Queen. Marowitz insisted that to do so would mean that the production would have only Six Deadly Sins and that the committee's suggestion seemed so incredible that he was unable to give it any real credence. The night of the premiere the press and the theatre's subscribers were in the audience. Shortly before the performance was due to begin the chairman of the management committee, Michael

Goldberg, rose to address the audience. He announced that the performance was to be cancelled due to differences between the director and the committee of management. He said that the director of the production had introduced an impersonation of Queen Elizabeth II personifying Sloth. This in the opinion of the management committee was needlessly and gratuitously offensive. Since the director was unwilling to modify the scene the management committee felt it had no alternative but to cancel the performance.

Marowitz, who was in the audience, rose and protested that what the management committee was doing was an outrageous act of censorship. Marowitz suggested that Marlowe's own intention with the Seven Deadly Sins had been satirical and that he did not see why he himself should not be allowed the same license which Marlowe himself used in writing the play over 300 years earlier. A senior board member shouted that the director should have some sense of responsibility toward the committee since it had rescued the theatre financially, a theatre that was losing money, and was dependent on public support. Marowitz responded that if they were to cancel the production it would only lose money for the theatre. Furthermore the Close Theatre was a club theatre created (on the model of the Traverse Theatre) with the original intention of avoiding the censorship of the Lord Chamberlain. Marowitz then walked out, declaring that he was quitting the production.

The following day the cancellation of the production was headline news in newspapers throughout Scotland and England. News of the cancellation appeared on the front page of *The Scotsman, The Glasgow Herald,* and the *Daily Mail,* among other broadsheet newspapers. There then followed a series of meetings between the theatre's directors, members of the board, and the chairman and Marowitz himself. At that point everyone was anxious to find a compromise, although Marowitz continued to refuse to remove the scene in question. Marowitz suggested that they replace the Queen's tiara with Britannia's helmet. This was the necessary concession that allowed the production to go forward. The controversy had the effect of generating a large amount of publicity which then led to a sell-out run. Ironically the controversy helped to enlarge the bank account of a theatre in need of box-office revenue at the time. During the controversy Marowitz demonstrated again his ability to hit a nerve centre of sensibility in Britain and thereby generate widespread discussion about theatre's boundaries which in turn has the potential to enact a degree of change.

London Traverse

The Glasgow Citizen's Theatre controversy was not Marowitz's first intervention in Scottish theatre. Following Marowitz's participation in the landmark *'Happening'* during the 1963 Edinburgh Drama Conference, he and Jim Haynes, who had helped sponsor the conference, began to collaborate. In 1964 Marowitz persuaded Saul Bellow to allow him to direct three one-act plays Bellow had written, at the Traverse Theatre club in Edinburgh. The programme became known as *The Bellow Plays* and later transferred to the Fortune Theatre in London. Also in 1964 Marowitz directed Jack Richardson's *Gallows Humour* at the Traverse during the Edinburgh Festival. In 1965 he also directed Peter Barnes's first work entitled *Sclerosis* and Peter Weiss's play *A Night with Guests* at the Traverse in Edinburgh (McMillan 1988: 105–110). As the previous chapter has outlined, Haynes believed that in order to maximise the trajectory of the Traverse's work, both in terms of prospective talent as well as finance, a London venue needed to be directly linked with the Traverse in Edinburgh so successful productions could transfer. After a prohibitively expensive season of work at the Arts Theatre Haynes relocated the venture to the Jeanetta Cochrane in London in 1966 and asked Marowitz to be associate director (Hewison: 1986: 112).

In 1966–1967 Marowitz directed Joe Orton's *Loot* at the London Traverse, which received the Evening Standard Award for Best Play of the Year. Previously the play had had a difficult run in the regions. Nonetheless Marowitz was approached by producers Michael White and Oscar Lewenstein about the play in 1966 while he was working as a director with the London Traverse. During the regional run the cast sensed that audiences were not engaging with the material and so they began to add one-liners and inject their own collective invention into the performance 'script'. When Marowitz was approached about doing the play at the London Traverse he asked to see the original version of the script and when he read it he was astonished by its sophisticated literary constructions and the subtle black comedy. He immediately agreed to stage the production during the London Traverse's first season and then worked on the script with Orton.

Marowitz's directorial approach to the play was to make social and moral excesses plausible, and to find the truth which lay deep within the material. The production opened in September 1966 and transferred to the Criterion Theatre in London's West End in January 1967. *Loot* ran for 342 performances (Shellard 1999: 127) but despite positive reviews the play continued to cause offended patrons to leave the theatre in the middle of the performance. Nevertheless the production achieved such a profile that during the West End run directed by Marowitz the producers also negotiated the film rights for the play. The production also became a point of reference during the 'dirty plays' controversy initiated by the impresario Emile Littler, a controversy based around collective hostility towards displays of nudity, promiscuity, and most of all the representation of homosexuality (Marowitz 1990: 104–105). This can be seen as evidence that Marowitz was involved with work that served to generate public discourse in Britain on controversial issues.

Ten months after the play opened, Orton was murdered in his sleep on 9 August 1967 by his lover Kenneth Halliwell who then committed suicide by overdosing on sleeping pills (Shellard 1999: 126). The murder-suicide was headline news and Marowitz was subsequently approached by numerous journalists and researchers interested in any insights he could provide about Orton. Although Marowitz and Orton did not particularly like each other on a personal level (Marowitz 1990: 109), they shared a similar irreverence and hostility towards the British establishment which found expression in their collaborative work together.

Open Space

In 1968 Marowitz opened the Open Space Theatre on Tottenham Court Road in collaboration with Thelma Holt (Hewison 1986: 200), described by Marowitz as a young actor and producer who had recently completed training at the Royal Academy of Dramatic Art (Marowitz 1974: 7–10). In fact, at this time, Holt (b. 1932) was a successful actor. One is reminded in this case of the necessity of cross-checking information given by interviewees, where memory may be faulty or information skewed by personal bias, lack of knowledge, or, indeed, affected by self-mythologisation. According to Marowitz, and verifiably, Marowitz first met Holt when she was acting in Leonid Andreyev's play *He Who Gets Slapped* at the Hampstead Theatre Club in 1964. Marowitz says he explained that he wanted to create a permanent home for a small resident company and mount experimental and unorthodox theatre and performance, including works which were not plays necessarily but collaborations collectively devised by a permanent ensemble. Holt was interested, according to Marowitz but only on the basis that she would have an active managerial role in the new theatre.

In fact, there was more of a time-gap than Marowitz remembered between the initial meeting and the opening of the theatre.

This is hardly surprising since the plans could hardly have been conceived on a first meeting after a performance when he first met Holt. The theatre actually opened four years after their first meeting and over the next twelve years the Open Space would become one of the leading experimental theatres in Britain and introduce new works by such British playwrights as Howard Barker, Trevor Griffiths, Howard Brenton, Peter Barnes, David Rudkin, John Hopkins, and Mike Leigh. The Open Space would also introduce new work to the British theatre by many important American playwrights including Sam Shepard, John Guare, Terence McNally, Lawrence Melfi, Charles Ludlam, Mike Weller as well as work by Jean Claude van Itallie.

During the first four years of the Open Space's existence from 1968 to 1971, nineteen out of thirty-three productions were American plays (Schiele 2005: 56). Marowitz was interested in utilising the best material from Off Broadway and Off Off Broadway. Such material in addition to being novel material within a British context, was also written to be performed in very similar conditions to those provided at the Open Space. In his introduction to *Off Broadway Plays 2* Marowitz explained that 'The Open Space Theatre rapidly became a kind of extraterritorial Off Broadway outpost.' (Marowitz 1972: 10)

In many respects the Open Space was an Off Off Broadway Theatre in London. It hosted an American season of plays in 1969 and continued to premiere many more American plays even to the exclusion of a number of talented British playwrights. Many of the groups explored throughout this book also performed at the Open Space, including La MaMa, Freehold, and Pip Simmons (Schiele 2005: 210–216). The Open Space was known for environmental pieces, Shakespeare collages, and premieres of new writing, including the world premiere in 1971 of *The Four Little Girls* by Pablo Picasso. This production is particularly interesting with regard to this study. Picasso and Artaud had been friends and Jinnie Schiele suggests it was this link with Artaud that, at least in part, piqued Marowitz's interest in the text (Schiele 2005: 53). If so, this interaction reflects a point made earlier that while this book deals with American influence on British alternative theatre, it also recognises that the interaction was two-way and that, within the general argument being made here, there has also to be recognition that European experimentalism was also an important contributor to British alternative theatre through such figures as Artaud, not to mention others like Grotowski and, later, Kantor.

The first production presented at the Open Space, however, was *Fortune and Men's Eyes* by John Herbert. The play opened on 10 June 1968 and was set in a Canadian reformatory. The audience was ushered in through a fire exit instead of the main entrance and walked in single file through a narrow passage way on the iron fire escape. A metal door was opened by an armed guard who took the audience's tickets while two inmates stared silently from behind iron bars as the audience entered. Another guard with a submachine gun supervised from above. The audience was fingerprinted, and then ushered into a cell until twelve people were in each cell. Meanwhile loudspeakers blasted announcements related to prison life until the sound of a shower and the appearance of the four actors who were central to the play marked the beginning of the performance.

The production was an attempt to break down the traditional barriers associated with a proscenium arch theatre and to implicate the audience directly in the action of the play. This can be seen as an instance of performance efficacy as the audience is made to adopt a role and is inculcated into a subjective view of a criminal justice scenario. This in turn had the potential to alter the individual audience member's view as it relates to the criminal justice system. Before the foundation of the Open Space Marowitz had repeatedly stated that, in his view, there was no theatre movement in Britain which could be described as avant-garde. His fundamental concern was with breaking down the conventional presentation of character (Schiele 2005: 111). The run of the play was extended at the Open Space until 4 October 1968. It transferred to the Comedy Theatre in London's West End on 17 October (Moffat 1978: 69).

The first productions of American plays at the Open Space were two one-acts both directed by Marowitz. The first one act in the double bill at the Open Space was *The Fun War* by Geoffrey Bush, the second was *Muzeeka* by John Guare. Both works were anti-naturalistic in their dramaturgical composition. *The Fun War* was about the Spanish-American War. At its heart it was about the origins of a tendency in American foreign policy which had arguably led to many subsequent foreign interventions including the conflict in Vietnam. *Muzeeka* had been an Off Broadway award winner in 1967 and was about a young man destroyed by American society, American materialism, and the Vietnam War. At the Open Space American national identity was directly challenged within a British context which had the potential to alter the British audience's view of political links or the 'special relationship' between the two countries at the time. After discovering that he enjoys killing, the young man then kills himself. These plays were indicative of Marowitz's practice of using the Open Space to introduce the work of Off Broadway and Off Off Broadway playwrights to Britain.

Works known as the Marowitz Shakespeare collages which were produced at the Open Space included *A Macbeth, Hamlet, An Othello, The Shrew, Measure for Measure,* and *Variations on the Merchant of Venice* (Marowitz 1978: 7–27). Marowitz's intention in creating these works was primarily to confront the substructure of the plays in an attempt to test or challenge, revoke or destroy the foundations on which classical plays were revered and accepted. To accomplish this Marowitz challenged Shakespeare's presentation of theme and character and altered it to suit his own interpretation or intentions. He objected to the reverence with which he believed these plays had been treated and endeavoured to extract something new and pertinent by breaking them into pieces and reassembling them in a particular way. Marowitz wanted to create a different vantage point and obtain an inside view of external developments which he believed would potentially alter the entire resonance of the theatrical experience. In challenging the institutionalisation of Shakespeare's canonical texts in Britain Marowitz sought to reinvigorate these works and redirect their potential efficacy within British culture and society in parallel with work his colleague Peter Brook was doing about the same time.

In addition to the Shakespeare collages Marowitz also adapted four additional works during his London period. Oscar Wilde's *The Critic as Artist* was adapted in 1971 and produced at the Tottenham Court Road space as was George Buchner's *Woyzeck* in 1973. In 1979 Marowitz adapted August Strindberg's *The Father* which was performed at the Euston Road premises, and *Hedda* based on *Hedda Gabler* in 1980 which was performed at the Roundhouse. Marowitz's collage work and adaptations were inspired by the work of William Burroughs whom he cast as President Nixon in *Flash Gordon and the Angels* in 1970 (Miles 2010: 293) and again as Judge Hoffman in *The Chicago Conspiracy* (1971) both at the Open Space. They were also indicative of his lack of reverence for the classics which may have been a characteristic of many British-born theatre practitioners. The productions encompassed many different themes but share a common characteristic theme: the struggling individual bound by the strictures of conventional society and isolated from the rest of humankind because of a desire to break free from it.

Both verbal and visual shock tactics were incorporated into performance as an integral part of the means of expression. Simple or bare sets were used to facilitate quick changes, and lighting was the chief means of design, suggesting a different realm or reality from the real world, as in the use of gauze curtains and lighting effects in the *Critic as Artist*. Such design elements were utilised to remove the audience from the performance scenario by creating a dreamlike quality within the environment. Marowitz created an important and characteristic emphasis on speed. Speed generated a film-like technique in which the production would switch from one visual image to another unexpectedly and without rational explanation. This was intended to expose, through external expression, what was happening in the mind of a particular character as in a Hollywood movie.

The first Shakespeare collage to be produced at the Open Space was *A Macbeth*. The Wiesbaden Festival offered the Open Space £2500 to take the production to the Festival on the 14th and 15th of May 1969. There was a cast of eleven and the production design identified no specific period or location. The Marowitz adaptation stressed the occult and redistributed dialogue amongst a smaller number of characters than the original Shakespeare version, a characteristic of all of the Marowitz Shakespeare collages. Marowitz incorporated scenes of black magic ritual, shaping such ideas from the original. Lady Macbeth became the head of a witches' coven. The stage was a triangular platform intended as an emblem as was the shape of the gibbet. The gibbet appeared with the effigies of certain characters during black magic ritual scenes with the witches (Ellis, 2003). The floorboards were painted black and drawbridge like structures were used for entrances and exits at the back of the stage. Here we have an example of 'laying bare' which—conscious or not on the part of the theatre practitioners involved—is originally drawn from a Russian formalist conversion of text in to a series of devices.

The Critic as Artist

Marowitz's 1971 adaptation of *The Critic as Artist* involved the addition of a dramatic scenario in which Oscar Wilde and Lord Alfred Douglas meet for the first time. The adaptation stripped away Wilde's original prose from the piece, leaving only dialogue. The rationale for this move was to compensate for the fact that Wilde's original was not intended as a piece of dramatic writing. The set was a Victorian sitting room and green carnations were handed out to the audience as they entered the theatre. Curtains made of gauze surrounded the space and, when lit, became transparent, giving a dreamlike quality to the production. Timothy West played the part of Oscar Wilde. The production was critically successful and ran for five and a half weeks.

The second original piece by Marowitz to be presented at the Open Space was *Artaud at Rodez* in December 1975 (Schiele 2005: 214). Marowitz drew upon information he had gained through research into Artaud's life and his interview with Dr. Gaston Ferdiere in 1966. Dr. Ferdiere was Artaud's friend and the man responsible for Artaud's treatment at Rodez where Artaud was hospitalised. The piece shows a man obsessed with a personal vision of what art in the theatre ought to be and who is driven mad by his inability to realise his vision. The play was dramatised as a confrontation between Dr. Ferdiere and Artaud himself. Dr. Ferdiere was portrayed as the personification of conformist values at odds with Artaud who was portrayed as the personification of the artistic temperament.

In 1970, during the Open Space's third year of operation, the theatre received £1500 (now worth roughly £40,000) from the Arts Council but was otherwise struggling financially. Marowitz and Thelma Holt decided to arrange film screenings of a new Andy Warhol film called *Flesh* about a male prostitute who is pressured by his wife to raise money for her lesbian girlfriend's abortion. Warhol was a popular sensation at the time. Marowitz and Holt believed that the film screenings would generate some much needed income for the theatre and also reflect Marowitz's interest in the American avant-garde and Greenwich Village experimentation. The film was screened three or four times daily for three weeks, starting in January 1970. On 3 February thirty-two police constables and a superintendent from Scotland Yard raided the Open Space during a scheduled screening and ordered the projectionist to stop the film. The film and projector were confiscated by the police as were the Open Space's documents, books, and receipts (Miles 2010: 292).

The following day the raid was headline news and there was shortly thereafter a debate in the House of Commons about the film, involving then Labour Home Secretary and future Prime Minister James Callaghan. Ultimately, the Director of Public Prosecutions advised the Metropolitan Police that a criminal prosecution with respect to charges of obscenity was not warranted. Nevertheless a magistrate's hearing on the lesser charge that the theatre had allowed members of the general public into a licensed club was allowed to go forward. The Open Space was fined £220 which was then paid by Andy Warhol himself in a gesture of public support for the theatre (Marowitz 1990: 143–145).

In 1976 The Open Space moved to temporary premises in a disused post office on Euston Road because the block of Tottenham Court Road where the original Open Space was located had been closed for redevelopment. The company responsible for the redevelopment promised to include plans for a new theatre for the Open Space to occupy on Tottenham Court Road upon completion. This promise helped to influence the Camden Council to approve the demolition, but there was no written agreement and the construction company subsequently failed to honour its spoken agreement

(Schiele 2005: 7). This, along with a confluence of other factors, principally including the departure of Holt from the Open Space, led to the dissolution of the Open Space and Marowitz's subsequent departure from the UK in 1980.

The split with Holt arose after Marowitz abruptly got married for the first time in 1976 to the model Julia Crosthwaite in a civil ceremony at St. Pancras Town Hall. He told Thelma Holt about it only one day in advance. According to Marowitz his new bride became involved with designing the snack bar at the new Open Space Euston Road premises but Holt was not properly consulted and this created tension and acrimony. Previously Marowitz had abruptly contacted Holt during her own honeymoon and she had returned early to work on behalf of the Open Space at his insistence. Also at this time Marowitz had materials intended for his and his wife's new flat diverted temporarily to the Euston Road premises which was also under construction. Although Marowitz did not misappropriate funds from the theatre he did use contacts the theatre employed to handle his own work and purchased his private materials at wholesale prices through those contacts.

One of the builders at the Euston Road premises was also an actor Marowitz had rejected at an audition at the theatre and who also happened to live with a reporter for the *Evening Standard* (Marowitz 1990: 216). An article appeared accusing Marowitz of impropriety and although the board subsequently found that there had been no misappropriation of the theatre's funds, a stigma remained. Thelma Holt resigned her post as executive director of the Open Space in June 1977. Although the theatre kept going for an additional two years following her departure this marked the beginning of end of the Open Space as Holt had effectively kept 'the wheels turning' of the organisation.

Without Holt, Marowitz found that he had alienated himself from a large number of people within the theatre community. After the closure of the Open Space he was unable to generate fresh artistic collaborations in Britain. These factors, along with the collapse of his first marriage, led Marowitz to leave Britain for California where he lived from 1980 until his death on 2 May 2014. During the period at the Open Space Theatre (1968–1979) more than 175 plays were produced. Many writers and directors, such as Sam Shepard and Mike Leigh (Hewison 1986: 204), who started their careers at the Open Space were to go on to have significant influence on the course of theatre history in subsequent decades.

RSC

Another underlying factor that may have led to Marowitz's decision to leave Britain was that he had come to be seen as difficult to work with by some influential theatre figures. In 1974, for example, Marowitz had been approached by Trevor Nunn to direct Philip Magdalany's *Section Nine* for of the RSC and accepted. *Section Nine* began at The Place in London and then transferred to the Aldwych Theatre in London's West End. The play was a farce about Watergate. It was well received but Marowitz clashed with the cast as well as the author. The conflict occurred because Marowitz felt that the play did not have an effective ending and so to provide one he introduced a series of cartoon slides showing different heads of state embracing one another as a means of putting a comic punctuation mark at the end of the performance.

One of the cartoon slides was a drawing of Queen Elizabeth II embracing Idi Amin, which infuriated Magdalany. Magdalany brought the artistic director Trevor Nunn into the dispute and the slide was removed upon the productions' transfer to London's West End without Marowitz's knowledge. Marowitz became incensed and in so doing alienated himself from Trevor Nunn. He became stigmatised as difficult to work with. *Section Nine* was the last play that Marowitz directed for the RSC although he was involved with an aborted production of Jean Genet's *The Blacks* in 1988 under Nunn's successor Terry Hands (Chambers 2004: 93). It seemed that his abrasive personality may have led to his burning of too many bridges although this abrasive tendency was intertwined with his view that artists are motivated by dissatisfaction with what proceeds them.

Conclusion

As things turned out Marowitz's London period 1956–1980 was the prime period of his artistic and intellectual vitality. By analysing the events in his career during this period this study has sought to provide an overview but also contribute a new perspective on this important figure in contemporary theatre. By examining the reception of events as they took place and artistic developments as they evolved this chapter has sought to explain the main elements of Marowitz's work and has examined patterns within his career which are relevant to fostering a comprehensive understanding.

These patterns were intertwined with his own personal journey as well as contemporaneous events. The main focus of this book is the period 1956–1980 which of course coincides with his period in Britain. As described in this chapter Marowitz experienced the advent of Off Broadway first hand as a youth in Greenwich Village and as a theatre critic for the *Village Voice* climbing fire escapes and attending unconventional performances in unconventional locales. His move to Britain during the watershed year of 1956 combined with his iconoclasm and his pattern of confronting established practices and institutions were perhaps in some way emblematic of the changes in the alternative theatre movement itself during this period.

In his interview (5 June 2011) Marowitz identified the end of a particular phase of experimental theatre work with the coming of the Thatcher government in 1979 and the subsequent withdrawal in 1980 of subsidy from a number of theatres (Itzin 1980: 158). 1980 was also the year that Marowitz left Britain and returned to the United States on a permanent basis after the dissolution of the Open Space and a split with his partner Thelma Holt. There is virtually no existing commentary related to Marowitz after his London period. 1980–2014 was a period in his career which warrants further examination as many of his books, plays, and directorial projects including the Broadway production of *Sherlock's Last Case* (1987), *Recycling Shakespeare* (1991), and his work with the Czech National Theatre (2005) all took place after moving to Los Angeles. Although it is beyond the scope of this book, further study in this area would posit key questions about the impact of working within different theatrical environments and would seek to place the whole of his theatrical influence in perspective, in a way which has not been done before.

Chapter Six: Nancy Meckler

Nancy Meckler and her company Freehold were among the first to utilise the Drury Lane Arts Lab. Meckler arrived in London in April 1968 after working at the La MaMa Plexus in New York. Meckler and her company Freehold were pioneers in using the body rather than words as the primary means of expression (Chambers 1980:106). Freehold would help to introduce 'physical theatre' to the British theatrical landscape and introduce a new kind of dramaturgy based on the physicalisation of language.

> For Meckler's style of theatre is based on the most vital concept evolved by the American avant-garde groups of the 1960s: the body as a supersensitive instrument of expression. Her style of theatre is making a direct attack on our most notable stage convention—namely, drama as literature. It is the body which has to bear the main burden of the theatrical expression involved: the text is often viewed as a disguised tool of repression. (Ansorge 1975:26)

Meckler originally came to London for a few months during 1960 as a part-time student at the Guildhall while still an undergraduate student at Antioch College. In 1967 she did an MA at NYU run by Richard Schechner during the same period when he was founding the Performance Garage which later became the Wooster Group. It was at this time that Meckler first became involved with experimental theatre. In the evenings she worked and performed with the La MaMa Plexus and saw the work of the Living Theatre and Open Theatre (Meckler 2012). Ellen Stewart was very supportive and she let the group perform at La MaMa. Meckler then endeavoured to return to London and was accepted to a one-year course at LAMDA.

After completing the course she remained in London intending to stay on a temporary basis but met her future husband, the producer and lawyer David Aukin, and began working with the

Wherehouse La MaMa Group in London run by Beth Porter. Meckler ended up staying in London and, when Wherehouse La MaMa was disbanded by Porter, Meckler continued to work with the nucleus of the group and renamed it Freehold. Both the Wherehouse La MaMa group and Freehold based their activities at the Drury Lane Arts Lab.

The obvious comment on this year's remarkable boom in experimental theatre is that we have contributed remarkably little to it ourselves. It now operates from about half a dozen centres in London and its development in provincial cities has rightly been called the "Arts Lab Explosion". And yet from the work I have seen, it seems less an indigenous growth than an extension of the American underground. One recent case is that of the new Warehouse Company who were playing in the Arts Laboratory earlier this month. Three of their members come from the New York La Mama troupe as you might almost have guessed from their programme (Wardle, *The Times*, 21 December 1968).

Meckler had a conventional theatre background and was an undergraduate student at Antioch College in Ohio, and did postgraduate training at LAMDA with an acting course in the Classics and Shakespeare. LAMDA had an 'American course' for overseas students. It was a one-year course called the D course. She was in London on the course for nine months but then stayed for an additional year because she had started undergoing therapy in England.

Originally when Meckler was an undergraduate student at Antioch College she spent a year abroad in France at a university in Besançon, in the Franche Comté. In the east of France, this was not Paris and she found the environment exceedingly dull. She wrote to drama schools asking if they would take her for a term and the Guildhall School of Music and Drama in London said that she could visit and audition. She auditioned and the Guildhall said that they could not accept her as a full-time student but that she could study part-time. So Meckler initially lived in England for three months and was a part-time student at the Guildhall taking three classes in 1960 (Meckler, 2012). Two years after she graduated from Antioch College, Meckler applied to LAMDA.

When she returned to America after completion of the course, a friend from LAMDA was in a small group in New York City started by Stanley Rosenberg, who had been with Eugenio Barba in Denmark. Rosenberg was starting a company called La MaMa Plexus and there were seven people involved. He introduced Meckler to Grotowski exercises, like 'the Cat' and other physical exercises. Most of the members of the company were working or going to school during the day, so they would meet at 3.30pm and stay until 7pm. Some of them were teachers, some were actors, and Meckler was then doing a new MA at NYU (Dramatic Theory and Criticism) with Richard Schechner. Schechner was starting the Performance Garage and he was creating *Dionysus 69* at that time. Meckler was exposed at this time to physical theatre, Grotowski, the Living Theatre, and the Open Theatre. When she did the physical exercises she found them interesting and felt more released as an actor than she had when studying theatre in a conventional way (Meckler, interview, 2012).

Meckler was in New York and wanted to work as an actress. She got a job as a production secretary for a year with the Broadway musical *Never on Sunday* (1967). Then she was in England briefly visiting friends when she met her husband David Aukin. They started dating in 1968 and Meckler thought she would stay for a few more weeks. However, she did not have any work in New York, and so she stayed and has never left. She says her choice was as casual as that. Aukin was a lawyer at the time and was busy during the day whereas Meckler was prohibited from working in Britain without a permit. Meckler searched to find out if there was any theatre she could get involved with. As discussed in previous chapters, there was a La MaMa company in London run by Beth Porter, who had been in La MaMa's *Futz* and *Tom Paine*. Meckler started meeting with the group and would work with them virtually every day. They would do physical exercises which Tom O'Horgan had taught them when he visited and worked with the company during the London production of *Hair* in 1968.

There was a falling out with Porter after she went to America to film *Futz* (1969). According to Meckler when Porter returned to London there was a dispute about using the name of the company, Wherehouse La MaMa. While Porter was away other members of the group wanted to keep working. Meckler started working on a project with them called *Alternatives*. According to Meckler when Porter came back from New York she announced that she was disbanding the company immediately although they had a booking at the Mercury Theatre for *Alternatives*. There were seven members of Meckler's faction who wanted to carry on and so they then adopted the name, Freehold.

When Meckler started there were relatively few well-established women directors. Joan Littlewood was one and Wendy Toye directed commercial theatre. There was also Jane Howell at the Royal Court. Further there were some distinguished women directors in regional theatre, for example, Joan Knight who after several years of success at Farnham took over Perth Theatre in 1968, becoming renown in that role. Nonetheless, Meckler has a sense that it was unusual for a woman to be a director. This, she says, is why she did not pursue it at first. She did not think anyone would take her seriously even if she did want to be a director. Paradoxically by her own account Meckler fell into being primarily identified as a director because people knew she had directed in New York and so they would ask her to direct various projects (Meckler, 2012).

Jim Haynes also supported Meckler and Freehold. They had nowhere to rehearse so they went to Haynes and asked for his help. He said that they could rehearse in the Drury Lane Arts Lab which, as noted in Chapter Four, he had opened in August 1967, although at that time it was very busy. Both Ellen Stewart of La MaMa and Haynes shared a common characteristic of being historically important facilitators of theatre. Freehold would warm up in the foyer and occasionally David Hare and Howard Brenton who had founded the Portable Theatre, and were working at the Arts Lab, used to walk through the foyer and chat with members of Meckler's company. One of Freehold's members was dating Max Stafford-Clark who was still involved with the Traverse at the time. Stafford-Clark invited Freehold to Edinburgh and so they took *Alternatives, Mr Jello* by George Birimisa, and Maria Irene Fornes's *The Life of 3*. Maria Irene Fornes is associated with both the Open Theatre and the Judson Poets Theatre and also founded The New York Theatre Strategy (1971) which helped develop the work of such playwrights as Rochelle Owens, Rosalyn Drexler, and David Henry Hwang. The Freehold production of her play was featured in *Vogue*.

Stephen Rea was in Freehold at the time and describes working with Meckler and Freehold as his real training, as opposed to his time at the Abbey (Rees 1992: 37–46). Freehold did physical training as well as political training. Rea was making a living because he was Irish and he would get acting jobs as an Irish actor. He came to Freehold and said that he did not want to play exclusively Irish roles. The members of Freehold all worked for no pay. However, according to Meckler life in Britain was much cheaper at the time and you could live on ten pounds a week, and that included rent and food. Freehold were deeply influenced by *Towards a Poor Theatre* and did actor based Grotowski exercises. They were inspired by the idea of the poor theatre and the idea of the actor being placed at the centre of the work. With Meckler's productions, the dynamism always comes from the actors and so she has never heavily incorporated multi-media elements such as video for example, because she believes it swamps the actors.

Freehold's work focused on the actor and rehearsals would emphasise psychophysical exercises designed to free the actor for the maximum facilities of expression. Workshop rehearsals would last from 11am until 5:30pm with one break of less than an hour. The morning sessions involved calisthenics, gymnastics, acrobatics, and psychophysical exercises. The 'Cat' exercise for example involved a sequence based on the movements of a cat waking up and stretching but then became more strenuous and involved head stands and somersaults. The exercise could be done in many different ways by focusing on different words while doing it. Different words were expressed in different ways and accessed different feelings and intuitive responses.

In another exercise the actors would work in pairs while sitting on the floor. One actor would attempt a non-verbal vocal sound in order to express a simple idea. When the actor had finished the other would reply in the same manner. At a certain point Meckler would instruct the actors to get up on their feet and attempt to convey the idea to their partner by movement alone. The objective was to embody the meaning abstractly in both sound and movement. Finally the actors were told to combine the movement and the vocalisation (Shank 1972:16).

In another exercise Freehold employed, which was also used by the Open Theatre, the group divided into two lines each facing each other. One person began a movement and a non-verbal sound which they repeated again and again as they approached a second actor in the line facing them. The second actor would then absorb and embody the sound and movement of the first actor who would then take their place in the line. Then the second actor would slowly change and evolve the movement and sound organically into something else and then repeat the process by passing it along to another company member in the line.

During the afternoon rehearsal session, Freehold would reassemble and work on developing their next production. The nonverbal sounds and abstract movements were now used to express images, feelings, and the prevailing environment of the work. This was the method used by Freehold even when the starting point was an established classical piece of literature (Shank 1972: 18). The objective was to eliminate the filter of the conscious mind between the stimulus and the impulse. During these workshop rehearsals Meckler would take notes on things that might be used in the production or which seemed to have the potential for further development. After a certain time Meckler would stop the exercise and there would be a general discussion about what had taken place. Then the same actors or perhaps different members of the company would repeat the same process with the same lines but focus on Meckler's directions or images which in the first attempt and, through discussion, seemed to yield the most interesting possibilities. It was Meckler who guided the actors and selected elements for the production; however, all of the members of the group contributed significantly and creatively by way of their improvisational work. In anticipation of a new piece Freehold would rehearse for approximately four months in this manner, five days a week.

Freehold's most successful work was an anti-war adaptation of *Antigone* (1969–70). It marked a shift away from purely conventional literary reinterpretation and involved physical gymnastics and an orientation based on the impetus provided by the Peace Movement in America. The company created non-naturalistic images through gesture and movement and changed the invocations to the gods into appeals for 'a commitment to Love' for example.

The contortions and physical images created on stage drew an analogy with classical choric laments. It was intended to resonate with the audience in addressing their own group dilemma as once the Chorus had done for Theban nobles. The actors were not tied to one consistent character as would be the case in a conventional narrative (Craig 1980: 106). Rather, this practice was Post-Brechtian and in keeping with contemporaneous work by the Open Theatre and the Living Theatre.

Antigone came about after Freehold had gone to the Traverse with *Mr. Jello* and *Alternatives*. They returned to London as the Drury Lane Arts Lab was in the process of closing down and so they found a room to rehearse in at the Oval House. They started creating *Antigone* because Meckler was fascinated by Greek tragedy. In New York La MaMa Plexus had often used scenes from *Oedipus Rex* for exercises. This type of work involved very lengthy improvisations in which everyone would act out their expressionistic subtext. There were rarely lengthy discussions but according to Meckler people would do inspired things, and other people would then feed words in. Although with *Antigone* they were assisted by the writer Peter Hulton, the members of Freehold all took turns typing up sections. The *Antigone* costumes were made out of Army surplus clothing, all dyed oxblood red (Meckler, Interview, 14 January 2012). This is how they created *Antigone*. Meckler would take it apart and get rid of sections, and then Hulton would write another section. Everybody contributed material, and then the company put it all together with the assistance of Hulton.

The Oval House and Peter Oliver who ran it allowed Freehold to rehearse there and he only charged them the equivalent of tube fare. They rehearsed *Antigone* there and the People Show and Pip Simmons were also working there. Then the groups also started performing there as well because it was free. It was not registered as a theatre at the time but as exclusively a youth centre. With *Antigone* there was a dismantling of traditional hierarchies, in terms of director, actor, playwright, and audience. The Living Theatre was a big influence and the members of Freehold saw the Living Theatre when they came to London in 1969. To a certain degree Freehold were imitating them and the Open Theatre: Meckler adored the Open Theatre, and although she did not know how they did what they did, on some level her company was emulating it and trying to understand it. One of the ways in which Freehold emulated the Open Theatre was by allowing process and technique to arise from the material.

The Living Theatre performed shows at the Roundhouse, such as *Frankenstein* in 1965 and, much later, *Prometheus* in 1979. By the end of *Frankenstein* some audience members would take their clothes off and then go out onto the streets. According to Meckler, people were high on drugs and they were saying things like 'theatre belongs to the people, come out and onto the streets' (Meckler, 2012). After the members of Freehold had been exposed to performances like that the conventional theatre seemed antiquated and very tame. Meckler and Freehold wanted to do this kind of work and to break down barriers. Freehold did not want sets and costumes or stars. Britain had had censorship until 1968 while Freehold's work was anti-establishment and responding to the hippie movement. It was anti-consumerism, anti-establishment, and anti-strait-laced parents (Meckler, 2012).

The Freehold *Antigone* was a deconstructed version of Sophocles' play and Meckler reworked the language so it would be more accessible and relevant to contemporary actors and audiences. Freehold rehearsed *Antigone* for three months and then performed it at the Drury Lane Arts Lab. Jim Haynes was very keen on *Antigone* and gave them space to perform. The group then managed to get a booking at the Edinburgh Festival, in the same tent as the People Show. It was a circus tent by day. In the evenings the groups alternated the six and the nine o'clock slot. Haynes was there with the organiser of an Arts Festival in Berlin who then invited Freehold to transfer their adaptation of *Antigone* to Berlin to open the Festival. And so, suddenly, Freehold were on a train to Berlin, opening the Arts Festival in a 600-seat theatre. When in Edinburgh Freehold also met Richard Demarco, who then invited Freehold to appear in his gallery with their production of *Antigone*. The production did not have a set and so they could perform it anywhere with very little set up required.

The Vietnam War was in the popular consciousness and Freehold's *Antigone* had key anti-Vietnam War overtones, as it is about a young man who lies unburied. Freehold, which received the John Whiting award for New Writing for *Antigone* in 1971, devised their text based on the original, altering, for example, one chorus to a chant: 'in the name of love for a country, a man has gone to war. In the name of love for a country, a brother is not buried' (Meckler, 2012). The idea conveyed was of people going to war because they do it in the name of love and yet that impulse is opposed by a forced neglect of family duties.

Freehold's work was expressionistic but not necessarily provocative in its approach to its audience. Freehold company members put their names in programmes but did not want anyone to know what parts they played and at the end of the play Freehold had a sequence where, as the body of the young man was not buried, the actresses took turns being the body at the front of the stage. Then, when Antigone came on, she buried 'him' by throwing bits of newspaper over him. At the end of the performance they had a box of the newspaper, and the audience were invited to take handfuls and bury the body by throwing newspaper on it. This was an efficacious performance practice intended to change the audience members' attitude and relationship to the war in Vietnam. Interestingly in England, according to Meckler, very few people in the audience would get up and participate, but in Germany the entire audience got up to do it and took it very seriously perhaps to do with more openness towards post-Brechtian ideas in Germany regarding experimental theatre.

Meckler had come to Britain in the year of the big Vietnam exodus in 1968. She did not come because of Vietnam, but it was the year when a lot of people left America because of Vietnam and because they did not want to fight in the war. A lot of Freehold's work was to do with the hippie movement and a generation in rebellion against their parents. 'Anything that came from your parents' generation, anything your parents would go to, you wouldn't go to. Anything your parents would wear, you would not wear. Anything they would value, success or careerism or having your name on a programme, nothing mattered except peace and love, and community' (Meckler, 2012).

Antigone was so successful and so lauded that in some ways it hampered the company because it could never quite achieve that level of impact again. With *Antigone* people started flocking to performances and fought to get in. There were never enough performances and the company was measured in terms of this later on This resulted in an expectation within the company of consistently trying to outdo their previous achievements. Because of the success of *Antigone,* Freehold was invited to tour widely with subsequent projects. *Antigone* went to the Venice Biennale, and another festival in Munich and was often revived. The British Council also sent them abroad. In the 1971 Zurich Festival Freehold performed *Mary Mary*. The companies that were in this festival included Teatre Libera, Living Theatre, La MaMa in New York, Cirque de Soleil, the Playhouse of the Ridiculous, Theatre National Strasbourg, Chelsea Theatre Centre, Bread and Puppet, and the Open Theatre. At that point Freehold was seen as being on the same level as these other historic alternative theatre companies.

Freehold was the first visiting company to appear at the Young Vic with *The Duchess of Malfi* (1970). Once again the clothes were all made out of army surplus and bandages. Freehold were attempting to be experimental and to break the mould and to go somewhere others had not gone. The goal was to deconstruct without a writer to help them. With *Antigone,* the writer Peter Hulton had assisted Freehold. However, with *The Duchess of Malfi* Freehold members were developing the working script themselves from a classic text. As such, they found themselves wallowing in the material and did not know quite how to shape it and effectively deconstruct the original material.

Meckler saw the Open Theatre present *The Serpent,* and she was fascinated by what they had done and how they had done it. Freehold attempted to emulate the Open Theatre in order to try and figure out how they did it. They did not know how else to find out because there was not very much written at the time about how the Open Theatre created and experimented. Freehold also attempted using exercises over and over again, hoping that something was going to be revealed to them and that it would open a door. This theatre practice helped evolve a new dramaturgy involving the deliberate breaking down of hierarchies. Many artistic movements react to what came before and that was true of the contemporaneous physical theatre movement of which Freehold was a part. The idea to physicalise language came out of a mistrust of traditional literary forms. This influence came from America through practitioners like Meckler, and groups in Britain then started imitating it.

In 1971–1972 Freehold presented *Genesis,* created in collaboration with the writer Roy Kift at London's Cockpit Theatre. The piece was clearly influenced by the work of Joseph Chaikin and the Open Theatre and in particular *The Serpent* which Meckler had seen in 1969. The actors transformed into animals and snakes and recreated biblical stories in order to show that man is the creator of his own myths and primitive notions of divine intervention and provenance stem from an impulse to supplant our feelings of guilt over societal transgressions and crimes. The piece began with a gymnastic display in which Adam and Eve evolve according to the modern understanding of biology rather than according to the traditional biblical narrative. Freehold's *Genesis* explored the murder of Abel by his brother Cain. In the Freehold adaptation it was Abel and not Cain who asks the question 'Am I my brother's keeper?' In the Freehold version brother murders brother out of frustration rather than jealousy.

Also in 1971–1972, *Mary Mary* was written for Freehold by Roy Kift and traced the history of the notorious 1968 case of Mary Bell from Newcastle who at the age of eleven was responsible for the murder by strangulation of a three-year old and a four-year old boy. The members of Freehold investigated her family background and aspects of her socialisation, growing up in poverty and the ignorance and amorality with which she was confronted from an early age. Bell's mother was a prostitute and Bell claims to have been abused by her mother as well as her mother's clients. As was the case with Freehold's work more generally, with *Mary Mary* the group was concerned with creating the physical reality and the aspects of perversion, oppression, and frustration which ran through Mary's experience of life. *Mary Mary* made a contrast with the company's other pieces which were on some level drawn from myth, ritual, and pre-existing classical texts. The story of Mary Bell subverts the mythic view of the young girl as nurturer. It is also worth noting that through trial and error Freehold made the decision to create these works in collaboration with a writer.

Freehold's exploration of the world of myth and legend was also evident in their final production, the 1973 adaptation of *Beowulf* adapted in collaboration with Liane Aukin and performed at the Traverse. This production was after Meckler had a baby and by her own account it was not a very successful production. There is a certain amount of risk in any theatrical endeavour, but in devising these kinds of works in particular it can potentially be a spectacular failure. In some ways, too, by this production, Freehold had become a victim of its own success. With public subsidy there also comes a certain compromise, Meckler argues.

As with the Traverse and many other examples, with public subsidy there develops the need for the conventional kind of administrative structure that, in turn, conventionalises the organisational bases on which the art is made. Then something is lost: a kind of anarchic ethos is gone. Once it is announced that a group will receive a sizable grant then it has to pay Equity wages. But once it has to pay those, Meckler argues, then it will not be able to produce the same sort of shows because the money will not reach far enough.

Paradoxically, when such companies were not paying anyone they could get twenty or thirty people or even more to participate (Meckler, 2012). Such a group could do all sorts of things like going into overtime without paying for it. To get public funding groups were obliged to be transparent and have certain administrative structures. In many ways this is a good thing but the point is that there is a certain trade-off that comes with public subsidy and the required restructuring of the organisation. There is at least a danger that the original creativity will be diminished or even lost.

There is a further potential problem because, when the Arts Council gives groups money, it also specifies, or at least this is Meckler's perception, that it must also tour for as many weeks as it rehearses. So, when Freehold rehearsed *Beowulf* for three months it was not a success but nonetheless Freehold was obliged to tour it for three months and in Meckler's view had no choice. After a while it became a treadmill and Freehold was obliged to tour shows that in their own view were not worth touring. Conversely, when Freehold started, people first became excited about the material and then a tour emerged out of a sense of building momentum and fully realising the project for its own sake. The work eventually became too much of a treadmill which is why, Meckler says, she finally bowed out and could not keep Freehold going after 1973.

It was an important feature of Freehold's work that they chose to focus on pieces revolving around dominant female protagonists such as *Antigone* (1969), *The Duchess of Malfi* (1970), and *Mary Mary* (1972). In fact this has been an important aspect of Meckler's entire career as a director in Britain since 1968. Meckler's other major contribution to the British alternative theatre during this period was in leading a group based in Britain which was doing work employing the very same techniques and practices as the Open Theatre, Living Theatre, and La MaMa. Her work then influenced the practices of future groups working within the British alternative theatre. Freehold also helped to nurture the early careers of such figures as Stephen Rea.

After Freehold Meckler also became very involved with Sam Shepard thereby providing another link with artists who began in Off Off Broadway. Originally Meckler got to know Sam Shepard because she knew his wife. She directed one of his plays and Shepard responded to her work. Subsequently Shepard and Meckler have collaborated on a number of his plays in both New York and London including the premieres of *Action* and *Killer's Head* in 1975, *Buried Child* in 1996 and the premiere of *A Particle of Dread* in 2014. Meckler was also the first woman to direct at the National Theatre's South Bank buildings when she directed Edward Albee's *Who's Afraid of Virginia Woolf* in 1981 (Hall 1993: 316) as well as directing new plays at the Royal Court, Bush Theatre, and the Almeida. It is necessary to point out that while her work was important to the alternative theatre movement in Britain in the late 1960s and 1970s the bulk of her career has taken place since 1980. She has also directed regularly for the RSC and from 1988 was Director of the company Shared Experience until it was disbanded in 2013. Shared Experience was founded by Mike Alfreds, an American director, in 1975.

Meckler's husband David Aukin was originally trained as a lawyer at Oxford but later came to be known as the 'King of the Fringe' when he was instrumental in founding The People Show, Joint Stock, Foco Novo, and Freehold, all four of which were run for a time from his and Meckler's basement in St. John's Wood. Aukin wanted to be a producer and at first what he did was to run Fringe companies. He administered Freehold and managed The People Show. He co-founded Joint Stock and also administered Foco Novo. In 1973 the members of Freehold staged a production of Chekhov's *Three Sisters* in Nancy Meckler and David Aukin's house and members of the audience would move from room to room. It was this production which inspired the beginning of Joint Stock (Susan Croft, UH, 8/4/2014: n.p.). Joint Stock was formed in 1974 by Max Stafford-Clark, David Hare, David Aukin, and, later, Bill Gaskill.

Aukin was also the director of the board of the Oval House and many of the alternative theatre groups migrated there after the Drury Lane Arts Lab folded in 1969. He later became, in turn, Director of the Hampstead Theatre Club, Leicester Haymarket Theatre, and Executive Director of the Royal National Theatre. He brought together a lot of the alternative theatre groups for a season at the Cockpit Theatre in 1971–1972 which included Pam Gems' first play. He was also responsible for bringing Joseph Chaikin and the Open Theatre from New York to play at the Roundhouse in north London in 1971.

Aukin produced the original production of *The Elephant Man* (1977) by the American playwright and co-founder of Foco Novo, Bernard Pomerance. It is arguably the most successful play to ever emerge out of the London fringe. Pomerance originally gave the play to Freehold but they did not know how to stage it without makeup. Eventually Pomerance gave the play to Foco Novo and they realised they could stage it using projections of original photographs of Joseph Merrick. They toured the production, directed by Michael Rudman, and played at the Hampstead in north London. Then it was performed in the United States at the Booth Theatre on Broadway and then again at the National Theatre in London. *The Elephant Man* was the longest running straight play in Broadway history and there was a recent revival which played on Broadway.

Conclusion

The influence of Meckler on the alternative theatre movement in Britain 1956–1980 was in the main two-fold. One aspect of her impact was that she and her company Freehold were important in introducing 'Physical Theatre', in a post-Brechtian sense, to the landscape of theatre and performance in Britain. Her other major contribution was in elevating the status of women as both directors and also as the primary focus of theatre and performance pieces. Although women represent half of the world's population historically within the theatre women have been marginalised. Although women were written about in ancient Greece they themselves did not write or act in plays and in England women did not appear on stage until 1661. It can be argued that literary 'Aristotelean' language itself has played a role in maintaining such a hierarchy. However Meckler's early career in Britain can be seen within the context of a generational shift which coalesced in Britain and America to a certain degree around the issue of Civil Rights, Women's Rights, as well as a reaction to American involvement in Vietnam. While her experimental role appears to have been fulfilled by 1973, her subsequent career has been highly influential and demonstrates how many 'Fringe' artists have become, over time, highly significant in the development and achievements of more traditional British theatre institutions.

Chapter Seven: Ed Berman

Ed Berman and his umbrella company Inter-Action Productions (legal entity Inter-Action Trust Ltd) were extremely influential in pioneering unconventional modes of community performance in unconventional locations for non-traditional theatre going audiences. Berman began as a playwright and in 1968 started the first permanent lunchtime theatre in the United Kingdom. Over the next decade his umbrella company and its components would be responsible for an extremely prolific range of community arts and professional theatre activities in dozens of venues. This included the activities of the British American Repertory Company. The British American Repertory Company was the first joint company approved by both equity unions in both countries and was designed for non-star actors and stage staff. Berman set up the British-American theatre company to create an exchange of actors and stage managers. The company was hosted by both the UK and US embassies on both sides of the Atlantic and so can be seen as reinforcing the 'special relationship' mentioned in previous chapters. They produced Tom Stoppard's *Dirty Linen* (1976) and *New-foundland* (1976), and *Dogg's Hamlet Cahoot's Macbeth* (1979). *New-Found-Land* (1976) is a comedy celebrating Ed Berman's successful application for British citizenship. There were restrictions in the deal, including a stipulation that British American Repertory Company could only perform in four theatres over two weeks in either country. This unfortunately meant that at the time the plays produced could only be seen by a small number of people.

In fact, Tom Stoppard developed several plays for Berman's theatres including *After Magritte* (1970), *Dogg's Hamlet Cahoot's Macbeth*, and the highly successful *Dirty Linen* and *New-Found-Land*.

When Stoppard learned about the work of Berman's Dogg's Troupe Berman told him that he, Berman, was Prof. RL Dogg who wrote for children. In libraries, therefore he would be found under "Dogg RL" (i.e. doggerel). This amused Stoppard and he wrote a piece for the company called *Dogg's Our Pet* (1971) and that began a ten year relationship between Berman and Stoppard. Stoppard developed scripts, culminating in *Dogg's Hamlet Cahoot's Macbeth* and *Dirty Linen*.

Structure was critical to the activities of Inter-Action and Inter-Action had the express aim of combining community work with professional theatre activities as a tool to change society for the better. The company had a charitable framework and its workers had a communal living arrangement which originally grew out of environmental concerns. Berman regarded the entire enterprise as profoundly political in terms of changing society but not in a party-political sense. Regarding the social and political function of his company's work Berman stated at the time:

> It's clear to me that if you accept the structure as 'political' as well as the intellectual and the verbal, then we are as 'political' as they come. 'Political' is not a code word for 'Marxist'. (Itzin 1980: 52)

In 1968 Ed Berman set up the charity Inter-Action. It became the umbrella for all his activities which included at least seven theatre companies, innovative community projects as well as initiatives making print and radio media accessible to local communities. Inter-Action also established the first City Farm and the first community architecture service in Europe. Berman has had a substantial and largely under-acknowledged impact on the British theatre landscape

Education and Early Initiatives.

Ed Berman was born in Maine and went to Harvard at the age of sixteen. His mother did not work and his father was an entrepreneur and salesman and owned an American-style drug store. Berman was offered a scholarship to Harvard when he was fifteen but was dismissed in his first year for checking out library books in the name of cartoon characters. McGeorge Bundy, the Dean of Harvard College, said that he was depriving his class mates of their books by returning them late. He studied Government and History, then Biblical Archaeology at the Divinity School. In 1962 he was awarded a Rhodes scholarship to study at Oxford but was thrown out of Exeter College as well. He was drunk a fair bit of the time and was also arrested during his first year in Oxford for fighting with another Rhodes Scholar during a trip to London (Berman, 2010).

At Harvard Berman became friendly with two Indian students and Berman edited one of their theses which later became a book on Gandhi's period in South Africa. The thesis opened his mind to apartheid and to Gandhi and remained an important influence on Berman's life and art—which in part is why he now goes to India for a few months each year to do charitable work there. During his youth Berman also spent time on a private Civil Rights tour of the US. He was interested in Civil Rights and hitchhiked through the South and Western United States. He was repeatedly thrown in jail for vagrancy (Berman, 2010). He found some of what he saw in the South and South West frightening and disgusting. Berman became deeply interested in civil rights issues and the suffering it imposes on disadvantaged populations. He became a volunteer for Philips-Brooks House (a student voluntary society) when he was at Harvard and went to South Boston to work with inner city Black youth. The experience became an important influence and he quickly came to appreciate how far removed his Maine upbringing and background was from theirs. He tried to find ways to deal with Black youth and their differences. He began to develop and use children's games in an adult format to engage with them.

This initiative was the beginning of what later became known as the 'Inter-Action Creative Game Method'. For example, Berman took the game 'Simon Says' and adapted it by tapping a rhythm. If this was followed by Berman raising a finger, the participants were to copy him. If he tapped and did not raise a finger and they copied him anyway, they were out. Berman was later to use this strategy as a training method for work with actors, young people, and psychologists. Berman used the Inter-Action Creative Game Method to train a range of different groups, including those with disabilities. He would do three or four sessions a week and train others to do the same. His game method was intended to help persons discover their individual creativity and their creativity within a group.

Berman read Government at Harvard and also learnt Turkish. At Oxford he studied the history of the Islamic peoples, but realised his interest was also in education. He shifted to psychology and education. Inter-Action Creative Game Method was quite developed by then and Berman wanted to study the roots of creativity. He started a D.Phil. at Oxford working on how new textbooks in countries such as Turkey, emerging anew, fostered completely new and radically different self-images of 'citizens'. Ataturk had discarded the old Ottoman Empire books of learning which were in Arabic and Persian and replaced them with new text books using the Latin alphabet.

Berman went to Turkey to pursue his research and lived on the Asian side of Istanbul, overlooking the Bosphorus. One day while reading on his balcony he was attacked by two neighbours on leave from the Turkish navy. They thought Berman was a spy and beat him severely. He was told that he had a clot on the brain and was given one year to live. Back in the United States authorities informed him that he could not return to Turkey because he had been accused of defaming Ataturk and the Turkish nation. Berman asserts that he still carries back injuries as a result of this incident to this day. It was also this incident which led Berman to start writing creatively (Berman, 2010). Berman had lost the stereoscopic vision in his eyes after the attack, and could only read in short bursts. He thought he had not long to live so he began writing plays on issues important to him. At first he scrawled them out and someone else typed them up because he could not see clearly. *Freeze* (1966) was about cryogenics, a family trying to freeze their grandfather. *Stamp* (1966) was about Vietnam and later the advertisement for the show was a facsimile of a dollar bill, asking 'Is this worth the price of murder and slaughter in Vietnam?' Berman returned to England in 1966 but left Oxford and his D.Phil. behind.

England and New Associations

Berman had left Oxford, and his girlfriend at the time suggested that he send his plays to Jean Pierre Voos at the Mercury Theatre, Notting Hill. The Mercury Theatre was the home of the Ballet Rambert Dance School and Voos's International Theatre Club was also based there at the time. Voos put Berman's plays on at the Mercury and made Berman a writer-in-residence. *Stamp* was also performed at the Little Theatre off St Martin's Lane in London. At this time Berman first met Chris Cooper when Cooper was an Arts Council officer. They later had a longstanding working collaboration, Cooper eventually becoming the manager of Inter-Action's ship, HMS President 1917, when he was made redundant from his role as Director of South East Arts.

During 1966 Berman was also involved with some 'legal' smuggling of Hellenic art from Turkey which took him to Sweden (because his co-smuggler had a Swedish girlfriend) where he met the La MaMa troupe. When Berman and La MaMa later met up again in London La MaMa agreed to perform one of Berman's plays, *Super Santa,* which was performed at the launch of the Kensington and Chelsea Arts Council Committee. At the same time he presented the La MaMa production of *Tom Paine* also at the Mercury Theatre in 1967. Berman remained friendly with La MaMa.

In London from 1966 onward Berman continued to develop the theory and practice of interactive games. Berman did this with groups of young people, actors, and community groups in London. In 1966 he was living on the floor of a flat rented by Voos and his wife Diane in Queensway. There he met Clive Barker from Birmingham University who had worked with Joan Littlewood and was also working with theatre games. Their work became mutually influential even though Berman was focused on the psychology and creativity of individuals and groups generally while Barker's interest was in theatre games more specifically. Working in a community centre called Beauchamp Lodge, which had a canal boat on the Regent's Park canal, Berman offered to use his Game Method with children. Together Berman and Barker did a piece about Beowulf and the Dragon on the canal boat. Clive Barker served on the board of Inter-Action from its founding in 1968.

Berman met a lady named Pamela Rose connected to those running the Rambert Company. Her husband, Jim Rose, was writing a book on race relations in the United Kingdom. He wanted to meet people working with people from diverse backgrounds and mixed groups. She was introduced to Berman. Jim Rose had worked on the Enigma project at Bletchley Park during the war and maintained many influential contacts from there, including Richard Marsh who later became the head of British Rail. Berman wanted to set up a charity for Inter-Action and wanted Jim Rose to be the

Chair but first Rose had to finish his book. Berman was doing volunteer work at the time, sleeping on floors, and receiving meals from various people.

Berman also became friendly with Junior Telfer in 1966–67, a West Indian who ran the Ambiance Restaurant at No1 Queensway. Telfer's business was not doing well at the time. Together Berman and Telfer decided to open up the downstairs for lunchtime theatre. Berman had nurtured the idea of doing theatre at different times of day for people with different work schedules. Inter-Action's Ambiance lunch-hour theatre club was started in June of 1968 downstairs at Telfer's Ambiance Restaurant (Itzin 1976: 5), and Telfer became a Trustee of Inter-Action. They presented theatre at lunch and also did an event at 6 a.m. at Billingsgate Fish Market, with the Dogg's Troupe. The Ambiance lunch-hour theatre club was central to the lunchtime theatre movement that became a burgeoning focus for new writing development in London from the late 1960s to the early 1980s. This venture was ultimately responsible for a hugely innovative programme of short plays by authors including John Arden, Heathcote Williams, James Saunders, Howard Brenton, Harold Pinter, and Tom Stoppard. It also introduced to the British theatrical landscape numerous writers from the new experimental theatre that had emerged Off Off Broadway during the 1960s. The Ambiance lunch time theatre did the play *The Electronic Nigger* by Ed Bullins in their first season and it caused outrage. Bullins was the cultural minister for the Black Panther movement. Berman's own first five plays were produced in 1966, 1967, and 1968 by the International Theatre club at the Mercury Theatre in Notting Hill. The group which formed around these plays decided to leave in order to establish new companies within the newly formed Inter-Action (Berman, 2010).

Inter-Action and its Components

Inter-Action became constituted in April 1968 as a Trust, then a company, both registered as charities. Jim Rose became Chairman and Coutts became their bank. The board included: Clive Barker, Jim Rose, Junior Telfer, and also David Henderson-Stewart, Berman's classmate from Oxford who was working for McKinsey & Co, and who brought in a number of people including the current Chairman (2014), Henry Strage, then a partner at McKinsey. Inter-Action brought together ideas and actions. Patrons became involved on the basis that they would assume a title, but with no commitment to attend meetings or to give donations. Stephen Pilkington invited Inter-Action to use his home at Rutherfield Hall for a summer residency in Sussex for a time during the late 1960s and early 1970s. During the first summer, John Fox, later of Welfare State, was based there.

Inter-Action also began a publishing company and community print shop. The publishing arm of Inter-Action was called In-Print and published books and booklets. One was authored by Andrew Phillips, later Lord Phillips of the Charity Commission, called *Charity Status and the Law*, and another was by Erin Pizzey on *Women's Refuges*. Additional titles included *Converting a Bus* about the Fun Art Bus; *Print, How You Can Do It Yourself*, teaching people how they could print for themselves; and *Tools for Change* and *Video and Community Work*. They published a series of handbooks which at first were distributed by a co-operative distributor, but when that failed they sold off some of the titles to the BBC and to other community publishers. They produced song books and tapes for the BBC entitled *Healthy Learning Songs*. They developed a vocabulary for teaching things like health to children with the idea that this way children would learn information for life. For each topic, say teeth-cleaning, they would have four different ways to learn: a song, a game, activity, and a game song. The books included playscripts, e.g. *Ten of the Best British Short Plays* and Tom Stoppard's *Dirty Linen* and *New-Found-Land.* Other books were intended for groups which at that time had no publications, such as *Battered Women and the Law.* These small publications for unrepresented communities identified issues which later became mainstream concerns.

In 1968 Inter-Action started working on a large derelict site in Kentish Town, London that had not yet been properly cleared. It was full of rubble and rats. They cleared the site and started a summer programme for children. The company took to building huge structures, like a Moby Dick. They told the children the story and built structures and then the children played around it. Berman believed that if you have an idea and it makes sense, you can find the funding. He set up and received funding for his City Farms, both by getting land from British Rail and money from the government's Urban Aid programme. It was the first time the Arts Council of Great Britain gave a Community Arts grant and Princess Anne also visited. Later Berman put in a planning permission request to convert Buckingham Palace into a youth centre.

Father Christmas Union

The Father Xmas Union was a component of Inter-Action and was set up in 1969 at the Oval cricket ground to stage large-scale social activist events such as a protest against the use of non-union labour by Selfridge's. The first Father Xmas Union event took place at Whiteley's Department Store in Queensway, London. Inter-Action was hired in the early 1970s to deliver the annual Christmas grotto. Father and Mother Christmases with Eskimos and penguins entered the store and began asking the customers what they wanted for Christmas from the store. The public began leaving the store with those goods. This made them realise that they had to consider very carefully what they chose to do as 'events' (Berman, 2011).

The Father and Mother Xmas Union next picketed Selfridges on Oxford Street and was arrested for blocking the pedestrian walk way. They had someone at hand to photograph the event. In the end they were fined £12 each. Their case was supported by Joan Littlewood and Vanessa Redgrave. The following year the company announced that the Father and Mother Xmas Union were going to attack Barkers department store where members of the British Army were demonstrating firearms to children in the Father Christmas grotto. Berman sent out a press release saying they were going to attack the British Army. The following day the British Army withdrew from Barkers.

Inter-Action's street theatre had core themes such as when they picketed outside Selfridges. The company was involved in direct action and were in and out of the courts as a consequence. A National Front man was standing for a seat on the Camden Council. Berman got a piano, removed all of the black keys, and delivered it to the man's front door with a corresponding note, and accompanying press release. The man did not win the seat, although this result was probably hardly a direct result only of Berman's actions. The Father Christmas Union was open to all and it also staged antinuclear performances. It was a clear example of the ways in which Berman's influence, derived from his experience in America led him to challenge and seek to affect cultural, political, and social attitudes through experimental theatrical methods and activities.

Ed Berman, the "Black and White Power Plays" Season, Roland Rees and Foco Novo

In a more apparently traditional theatrical context, Berman programmed the first innovative season of plays exclusively on

Black issues in Britain. The 'Black and White Power Plays' season was staged at the Ambiance in 1970. Non-theatre based and theatre based activities complemented one another in Berman's community focused experimental alternative approach. Berman and his Dogg's Troupe were involved with a Black Power event at the Roundhouse. Then Berman set in motion his Black Power Season of plays at the Almost Free. The 1970 season introduced the work of African American playwrights Ed Bullins as well as LeRoi Jones alongside work from white playwrights on Black issues by David Mercer and Israel Horowitz. As mentioned earlier, Ed Bullins, 'culture minister' of the Black Panther movement in the US, came to London and his play *It Bees Dat Way* was performed as a part of the Black and White Power Season. Roland Rees directed some of the plays in the season and went on to introduce the work of more new Black British playwrights with his own company Foco Novo.

Roland Rees had been in New York from 1965 through 1967 when theatre was being performed in all sorts of unconventional venues and he saw many practices that he had never seen before (Rees 1992: 16). In Greenwich Village he saw a lot of work at La MaMa as well as the work of his greatest hero, Joseph Chaikin, at the Open Theatre. Rees was interested in the form of Chaikin's work and the way actors played a number of different parts almost at the same time even as a number of different plots were going on simultaneously. Chaikin started his process by devising physical work with the actors in ways which Rees had not encountered before. Rees also saw Ellen Stewart produce unusual plays at La MaMa and he subsequently premiered plays by Rochelle Owen (who was with La MaMa at the time) when he returned to London.

> In 1965, America, and New York in particular, was the place where major cultural and artistic upheavals were happening. Experiments in film, theatre, the visual arts, contemporary music, and the fusion of these forms, the

> proliferation of new centres for their performance, the mushrooming underground presses, the organisations surrounding the Vietnam War demonstrations, the rent strikes, Black consciousness groups, the Feminist movement, and experiments in collective and personal lifestyles, all made a lasting impact during my two years in that city. The energy of New York taught me that you can step out of tradition, start your own and 'Go for it!' I did not need much nudging to give up my academic future and start work in theatre (Rees 1992: 16).

When Rees returned to the UK he became associated with Ed Berman's Almost Free Theatre. As mentioned above, Berman and Rees also did Ed Bullins' play *The Electronic Nigger* in 1968 which Rees had brought back from Harlem. The play had been performed in Harlem by the Black Arts Rep and the Negro Ensemble Company and Rees met with Bullins and asked him for copies of his plays which had not been published at the time. In 1970 they collaborated again on the historic 'Black Power' season which concentrated on Black themes and the work of Black theatre makers. One of the shows they did during the season was *Black Pieces* by Mustapha Matura. *Black Pieces* was composed of six short plays and Rees used Chaikin's method of melding the pieces together. One immediate consequence of the 1970 season was that Matura was commissioned and then became a leading writer.

At the end of the 1970 season a meeting was held to discuss the allocation of funds into promised Black projects. £300 had been gathered from a separate collection at the theatre. Present at the meeting were: Michael X, eventually the last man executed in the Commonwealth in Jamaica, John Arden, Ed Bullins, and Berman. Michael X said he was going to take the money and put it into a 'Black Bank'. None of the others would back Berman in his objection to this, leaving open the possibility of misuse. After the Black Power Season Berman set up a caucus so that other seasons could be established. Most notable were the Women's Season and the Gay Season because they would help to establish a pattern of identity-based performance characteristic of later alternative theatre in Britain during the 1970s.

It is clear that much of the efficacy under discussion arose out of interactions within networks of experience and influence. For example, as we have seen, Roland Rees, Bernard Pomerance, and David Aukin founded the Foco Novo Company in 1971 when they produced Pomerance's play of the same name. Pomerance who later wrote *The Elephant Man*, one of the most successful plays to emerge from the London Fringe, came to the UK from the United States in 1968. The first professional production of his work took place at one of Inter-Action's theatre sites and it was at Inter-Action that Pomerance met both Roland Rees and the producer David Aukin. By a strange coincidence Pomerance had gone to High School with David Aukin's wife, Nancy Meckler.

Foco Novo sought to find a new model of performance and to open theatre to new audiences in collaboration with the Labour movement, colleges, and theatres. The company also worked with trade unions and in particular the National Union of Mineworkers. Foco Novo performed different shows in different types of venues, including the Almost Free theatre in 1974 with the first British production of a Fassbinder play (*Cock Artist*), but preferred venues suitable to the particular project. It also toured with Brecht's *Man is Man* in 1975. Foco Novo preferred to play in unusual places but funding came with touring and a somewhat prescribed choice of work. Foco Novo's working process resembled Joseph Chaikin's, another example of an American nuanced network of influence, in that it favoured multiple narratives and an equal distribution of male and female parts on stage. Those choices defined the use of actors and also defined the use of characters on stage as differentiated from the use of both in a conventional play. Hardly any one character was dominant.

Separation

Berman was the Artistic Director of the Ambiance and Dogg's Troupe at the same time. Voos became paranoid, according to Berman, about Berman wanting to take over his theatre club at the Mercury. An Israeli man named Naftali Yavin had written to the theatre club while he was in Manchester doing postgraduate studies in theatre. Berman went to meet Yavin, and after seeing his work suggested to Voos that they invite Yavin to work with them at the Ambiance. Meantime, Berman had a falling out with Voos regarding their disagreement about control and felt it was necessary to leave. He took with him people from the company to do the new work he wanted to explore and develop.

Berman and Yavin began The Other Company (TOC) together in 1968. All of this happened within a few months (Berman, 2010). Yavin was interested in the Inter-Action Creative Game Method. Yavin later directed Berman's plays *Sagittarius* and *Virgo*. *Virgo* had a woman in a cage and dealt with issues of female beauty being either inside or outside. The cage rocked back and forth over the audience. Berman's interest was in exploring the relationship between action and the audience.

Berman developed his idea of 'environmental' theatre dealing with location and time while Yavin worked in powerful dramas by Peter Handke and James Saunders and devised work with the The Other Company. Berman created a formula for what he referred to as 'participatory theatre.' He would grade the shows on a scale of 0 (where the audience is seated watching action) to 10 (where the audience improvised the whole piece). His plays were developed along these lines and with reference to these criteria. In *Sagittarius* the actors sat on blocks surrounded by the audience. The play was about a dysfunctional family. Drawing upon and applying psychological games theory in a theatre context created efficacious environmental physical pieces. Yavin died tragically in 1972 of a drug and alcohol overdose on the same day that the Fun Art Bus was launched.

The Ambience in Exile

Later Telfer went out of business and the Ambiance, then called the Ambiance in Exile, moved to the Green Banana restaurant in Soho and then to the Institute of Contemporary Arts. At the Ambiance in Exile at the Green Banana, the theatre space was downstairs, down a circular staircase. If a box set was required it had to be brought in early in the morning and removed after the lunchtime show to make way for the evening's entertainment. The Green Banana space seated thirty to fifty depending on the configuration. Berman solicited new scripts and wrote his own. Berman met director Geoffrey Reeves through Barker and brought him Stoppard's *After Magritte* which they did at the Ambiance with a box set, with a daily get-in and get-out at the venue. Stoppard came to see his play and Barker acted in it and so did Prunella Scales who later became an Inter-Action Patron. Berman would ask anyone to do anything, under his 1 in 3 rule: if you produce something you need to have either a well-known playwright, actor, or director and you will probably manage to fill at least thirty to forty seats per show.

Berman found a workshop space for the Ambiance in Exile for free, for a time, opposite the Roundhouse. The members of Inter-Action began working with local children. Arnold Wesker was trying to get Centre 42 at the Roundhouse up and running during the same period as Berman was starting his work in Camden. Outside of the Roundhouse Wesker put up a sign saying 'We need £190,000'. Outside Inter-Action's workspace on the windows opposite the Roundhouse a notice read, 'We don't need £190,000 yet'. At this time Inter-Action also occupied up to fifty derelict houses in the area of Chalk Farm and West Kentish Town. They started by squatting which then led to them being given permission to occupy the empty council houses officially for 50p a week. This experience showed Berman how building and planning permission worked.

In 1971 Ed Berman moved the Ambiance Lunch Hour Theatre Club to an old electronic bingo hall in Rupert Street in London's West End and renamed the theatre club the 'Almost-Free Theatre' (Itzin 1976: 5). The Almost-Free Theatre staged seasons including the first season of Gay plays in Britain and the first season of Women's plays since the Suffragette era. There was also a season on anti-nuclear themes. Berman wanted to promote what he referred to as 'libertarian' theatre on Black power, women's rights, and gay rights for groups who did not have a theatrical voice at the time.

Audience members were asked to pay what they could or at least one penny, but there was no upper limit, so admission was almost free. The ground floor seated sixty, or alternatively, one hundred if standing. The Almost Free Theatre did lunchtime and evening shows. Early productions at the Almost Free included Peter Handke's *Offending the Audience*, and a T.O.C. production of a piece about the My Lai Massacre called *Games* by James Saunders.

Equity approached Berman and Mike Leigh to help unionise the Fringe. They drew up a proposed contract of work which Equity agreed to but when Equity tried to get Berman to apply it at the Almost Free Berman said he could not because the principle of the Almost Free was such that they could never guarantee making enough money to pay their employees Equity rates. All the actors shared the box office takings at the Almost Free. The stage-management crew, who were part of Inter-Action, were paid by the Arts Council grant the usual Inter-Action rates (originally a pound a day), plus housing, communal meals, and expenses. Almost Free productions were artistically important and showcased a long list of up and coming directors, playwrights, and actors all made possible by Berman's 1-in-3 rule mentioned previously. This was Berman's justification for not paying Equity rates.

Berman was also a part of a local campaign to stop Joe Levy (of D.E.N. and J. Levy), who had bought up a lot of the property around Piccadilly Circus, from developing a high rise office complex. The campaign was ultimately successful and was supported by local businesses. Berman's Dogg's Troupe staged street theatre and community events and performances on local issues and larger concerns working especially with children and families, as well as in hospitals, old people's homes, and other community venues. Dogg's Troupe was a versatile improvisation and performance group which was a key component in many projects. The core members were Berman, Patrick Barlow, Jeff Hoyle, and Jim Hiley. Harriet Powell, later with Spare Tyre, was their musician. One of their themes was being twice two-faced and the troupe had headdresses with two faces going backwards, and one face going forward, plus the actor's own face.

In 1971 Berman negotiated with British Rail to take over several tracks on 10,000 acres of British Rail-owned land. The land was deemed unusable for development under modern planning legislation because of its proximity to the railway lines. Inter-Action established the first City Farm in Britain in Kentish Town North London. The farm was originally called the Fun Art Farm and rapidly became a model for city farms which sprang up across the country. As with most of Berman's initiatives the farm was intended as a model that could be recreated elsewhere. At one point there were over 200 such city farms throughout Britain based on Berman's original model. Members of Berman's Inter-Action lived and worked collectively at the Farm, and, importantly, were early environmentalists. When the organisation grew, Berman negotiated to take over more housing from Camden Council. Members, including Berman himself, lived communally and were paid equal, low wages.

In 1972 a Routemaster bus was converted to create a small theatre on the upper deck along with a cinema showing short films and slide-shows downstairs. The Fun Art Bus was inspired by the idea that theatre should interweave itself into the normal everyday movements of people. Mimed vignettes were acted out in the windows when the bus pulled up to a normal stop along a given route. Liz Leyh painted a picnic on the top of the bus so that it could be seen from above from the windows of tall office buildings and housing. Plays were shown upstairs in the smallest proscenium-arch theatre in the world. The sides of the bus were brightly painted with slogans and pictures of the passengers on the upper deck. The Fun Art Bus visited communities all over Britain and went to the Munich Olympics in 1972. It also participated in community festivals and toured Britain and Europe. The adverts were comprised of cartoons and there were sculptures in the luggage compartment. The tickets were poems by such poets as Roger McGough and Adrian Mitchell and short plays were also performed by T.O.C. and the Dogg's Troupe.

Women's Theatre

The 1973 Women's Theatre Season introduced works by American writers including Sally Ordway, and new British writers such as Pam Gems and Michelene Wandor. Originally Berman approached a woman's street theatre group called Punch and Judy's because he wanted to organise a woman's play festival at Inter-Action's Almost Free Theatre. The lunchtime season of plays which followed in 1973 featured exclusively women playwrights, directors, and performers. The women involved decided to work in an unconventional anti-hierarchical manner by contrast with the patriarchal/hierarchical manner they felt was a characteristic of a male-dominated commercial theatre establishment.

Women at the time were primarily only seen as 'actresses' and very few women with the notable exception of those mentioned in the previous chapter were involved in the technical and directing side of theatre production. Berman convened a caucus for those who were interested in the development of women's theatre. Initially meetings were held every Sunday for a period of six months, meetings open to any woman who was interested in participating. Scripts were read and discussed. The women worked out the details of the season of plays for themselves and individuals were nominated to shadow those who were already working with the Almost Free. Women chose the plays but Berman reserved the right to the final selection in order to meet and maintain the necessary requirements for the continuation of Arts Council funding. His principles were strong, but he found he had to compromise them from time to time in face of the realities of organisational need.

Pam Gems and Michelene Wandor were involved in this process as well as many other women. Women directed, stage-managed, and administered the season thereby also helping many of them to develop their careers. This season led in time to the formation of the influential theatre company Women's Theatre Group as well as to Monstrous Regiment. Women's Theatre Group immediately began work on a new play about three Portuguese women who had been persecuted for their progressive work on women's issues (Itzin 1980: 231). Plays produced during the season included works by Jennifer Phillips, Pam Gems, Michelene Wandor, Sally Ordway, Dinah Brooke, and Jane Wibberley (Itzin 1980: 231).

Old Age Theatre

In 1973 Berman's company established the Old Age Theatre Society or O.A.T.S.. The Old Age Theatre Society came about because Inter-Action was approached by MIND to do some work in an old people's home. Inter-Action gave out cameras and encouraged the residents to go to places they were not normally allowed and to take photographs of each other. The project was very successful and Berman noted that a team of four of the residents could function very well as a unit. Berman suggested to the organisation that they go on a tour of old people's homes and lead similar-styled workshops. MIND refused because they said that the older people would not be able to do such a thing. Instead Berman got another group from Inter-Action to go in and do entertainments. He felt that it was a worthwhile exercise but not as potentially productive or empowering as allowing the older people to lead the work themselves (Berman, interview, 2010).

Gay Theatre

Ed Berman facilitated caucuses of individuals who identified with women's and gay theatre in an effort to establish seasons of both. Those assembled worked out various roles themselves, shadowing Inter-Action staff where necessary.

In 1975 there was a season of Gay plays including work by Robert Patrick, Martin Sherman, and Lawrence Collinson. It was the first such season of plays to be staged in Britain. The season led to the formation of gay theatre companies, principally Gay Sweatshop, Britain's first gay and lesbian theatre company (Itzin 1980: 234). Gay Sweatshop was a group of openly gay people who formed a professional theatre company which was possibly the first of its kind in the world. The aim of the company was to present material by the group that would liberate and not oppress. The aim was to make heterosexuals aware of the oppression they exercise and tolerate. The group intended to expose what they saw as media misrepresentations of the homosexual community and increase general awareness of the oppression of sexuality. Gay Sweatshop consisted of six individuals who performed, directed, and administrated the group, and ten voluntary helpers who included back stage staff. Gay Sweatshop toured England, Scotland, and Wales and performed both lunchtime and evening shows at Berman's Almost Free Theatre and the Institute of Contemporary Arts. All of their plays dealt with various aspects of gay people's lives in a truthful and non-stereotypical manner. Berman published the season of gay plays under the title *Homosexual Acts.* Gay Sweatshop was eventually disbanded in 1997.

1976

Ed Berman became a British citizen in 1976 and then received an M.B.E. in 1979.

In 1976 Berman produced a season to mark the American bicentennial. Berman asked Tom Stoppard to write a play for the 1976 season and he wrote *Dirty Linen* and *New-Found-Land* about Berman himself becoming a British citizen. The production was very successful and transferred from the lunchtime venue to the Arts Theatre in London's West End where it ran for four and half years. Berman also directed *Dirty Linen* and *New-Found-Land* in Chicago and on Broadway. Inter-Action greatly benefited financially from the tours of *Dirty Linen.* Funds went straight back into the company coffers. Rochelle Owen's play *Homo* was also part of the season. New plays were contributed by Mike Stott (*Lenz* adapted from Buchner), Henry Livings (*Daft Sam*), Wolf Mankowitz (*The Irish Hebrew Lesson*), and Edward Bond (*The Bundle*).

By 1976 Inter-Action was established and doing all original work. The company received funding from the Arts Council because of the serious nature of T.O.C.'s work. At the National Theatre's new South Bank building opening in 1976 Sir Peter Hall asked Berman to provide entertainment outside of the theatre. The Dogg's Troup did Stoppard's 15-minute *Hamlet* and also had a 'Community Media Van' stationed there. They performed three to four hours a day outside the National Theatre. An actor playing Shakespeare was on hand. He gathered volumes of Shakespeare text and cut them up into one-inch squares, signed them, and sold them off.

Technicians and administrators were core members of the Inter-Action co-op. Berman was Artistic Director and chose the plays and developed the Almost Free 'seasons' except for the Dogg's Troupe and T.O.C. productions which other colleagues directed. They attracted plays from Stoppard, Bond, and Arden and leading actors wanted to work with them because of the quality of the plays. They did only British or World premieres and Berman was interested only in new work and not classical theatre. Berman helped produce a staged reading of the *Non-stop Connolly Show* (1976) in London, after it had shown in Dublin, although in Britain most producers had been reluctant to touch it because of the extreme political views of John Arden and Margaretta D'Arcy.

Berman had good relationships with both Tory and Labour councils who helped Inter-Action to purchase properties for very little money. Inter-Action moved to its new location in Talacre Road, Kentish Town in 1976. The site was derelict but had been developed with sports and sitting-out areas where groups could do plays. It had been an old factory sweatshop from early in the twentieth century. Productions were rehearsed at the Talacre Road facility before transferring to the Rupert Street venue to perform for the public.

Berman wanted to build a permanent centre and the Talacre site had not been touched since the end of the war. He put in plans and got permission to develop the site in 1976. Berman used the designer Cedric Price and it worked out well although there were some defect issues which had to be resolved. The Centre was opened by Princess Anne. It had big open spaces and located down the road was the City Farm, free school, and housing association.

The City Farm was run at that time by Berman as he was living there. There was an old timber shed turned into a riding school and a garage which was turned into a workshop. There had been allotments in the area previously and stables for the horses to turn the locomotives in the Roundhouse around so it did not take much work to re-engage these buildings and their potential. The indoor riding school was for disabled children and local people took the old allotments. The local people kept goats, chickens, and made yoghurt but they did not have cows because it was illegal to do so in the city. However they built concrete cows and horses for the local children to play on. Some horses were donated and some were liveried for locals and some were bought. Other City Farms opened up and they established a National Association of City Farms which they ran for a year before it devolved. The initiative was helped when British Rail agreed, as mentioned above, to release land for the City Farms project.

Inter-Action was set up as a co-operative, based on environmentalism and the collectives' ideals at the time. The operational rules were agreed and set down by everyone involved but over time the number of rules became almost impossible to work within. The utopian concepts were not really possible to attain in an urban environment. There were too many distractions in the city with new people coming in with new ideas and with relationships from the outside. Housing was also a problem and although they had ten houses the situation was not sustainable when children entered the situation. For example, the members of the collective were committed to mutual wills, inheritances, and wages but in practice when someone inherited some money they tended to leave the co-op rather than part with it. Liz Leyh the sculptor put forward a motion that all of the women should have children at the same time so that the community could build a free school around them. The motion was passed but naturally the goal was impossible to achieve.

The co-op members on the whole were in their twenties and many had just finished university. Everyone lived and worked together but there were also Associates who came in to work but lived outside. The group was thought of as left-wing but they primarily thought of themselves as environmentalists. Everyone did their share of the cooking and cleaning. A fee of £1 per week was charged for room and board which later rose to £1 per day. The rule of thumb was that no-one ever earned more than an Unemployment Benefit within the co-op. If people earned money from outside work they had to pool it within the co-op. In the end it was impossible, according to Berman, to remember the rules as there were so many of them. When Berman left in 1985, one of the last to leave, he had no cheque book, savings account, pension, or credit. He then learned how to earn money through dealing in property.

Conclusion

Berman's contribution to British alternative theatre includes introducing the work of a wide variety of new playwrights, actors, and directors, many of whom went on to great prominence. He expanded the diversity of voices represented through his seasons at the Almost Free Theatre, inspiring the creation of many of the theatre groups which participated in the identity based theatre of the 1970s. With his lunchtime theatre, the Fun Art Bus, and other initiatives he made theatre available to new audiences and bridged the boundary between life and art. Finally, much of his work was socially and politically active. With the city farms initiative he introduced a new form of environmentalism to British society.

Berman spent thirteen years (1967–1980) working in theatre, half the time on community and educational work. When he saw the opportunity to expand into film, publishing, or video he would do so. He was interested in finding different ways for people to express themselves, especially those who seemingly had no voice. The Community Media Van was a good example of this. It had a radio telephone and went around Britain locating itself in public places. The telephone was connected through to leaders of local communities and members of the public were invited to speak to them about their grievances in public.

Since 1980 Berman has worked in Hong Kong, Germany, Holland, Norway, Sweden, South Africa, and India as a director and trainer. He advised Yale University on developing new social enterprises. In Russia he worked as an adviser to three State Ministers. In the UK he has served as a non-party political special adviser on inner-city matters to Cabinet Ministers including Michael Heseltine and Tom King. Among many other activities Berman was the chairman of the successful Save Piccadilly Campaign. He continues to spend part of each year in India advising on social enterprise projects, mainly with women, and on environmental projects especially in the area of water development. His lasting contribution to alternative theatre in Britain, however, surely lies mainly in the large number of companies and artists whose futures were founded on his open-minded encouragement and producing skills at Inter-Action, his conception of the need for inclusiveness, his ability to work across established social, cultural, sexual, and gender boundaries and his vision of the arts as central to community feeling, and health,—and fun.

Chapter Eight: Conclusion

> I must say it's pretty dreary living in the American age—unless you're an American of course. Perhaps all our children will be Americans.
> *Look Back in Anger* (Osborne 1956: 6)

The case has been made that American influence on the alternative theatre in Britain 1956–1980 was substantial. This chapter summarises the history of transmission in this area between the theatres of both nations, considers performance efficacies evident in that history in relation to literary theory in play during the study period, and concludes with questions of nationhood in relation to innovations in alternative theatre practice. It identifies and details defining characteristics of American influence during this period and, in doing so, seeks to establish credibility for the claims presented.

A History of Influence

The data for this book has been collected through interviews, archival work, and a review of existing literature on post-war British theatre including the alternative theatre movement. The main historical developments or phenomena referred to are the activities of the experimental theatre groups associated with Jim Haynes, Charles Marowitz, Nancy Meckler, and Ed Berman, four expatriate American theatre practitioners living in Britain during the time period 1956–1980. In addition this book examines important American based groups, Living Theatre (1947), Open Theatre (1964), La MaMa (1960), and Bread and Puppet (1965), which performed in Britain and which made an impact during the same period.

In addition a wide range of indigenous British groups, Pip Simmons (1968), Foco Novo (1972–1989), Joint Stock (1974–1989), as well as institutions, RSC (1961), Royal Court (1956), and individuals such as Max Stafford-Clark and in passing Thelma Holt, John Arden, and the Portable playwrights (1968–1972) which in one way or another were influenced by American exemplars. This study has described a collection of American experimental theatre and performance practices which came to influence the practices of the alternative theatre movement in Britain. Alternative theatre rejected the beliefs and expectations of traditional audiences and radically altered both the aesthetic and organisational basis upon which performance was created and its approach to and impact on cultural, social, and political perceptions.

The opening chapters provided background and context for certain patterns that would later indicate American influence on the alternative theatre movement in Britain 1956–1980. They argued that theatre has often been used to define or challenge national values and the notion of the nation. Particularly at times of national crisis the theatre has served as a political and ideological tool to help reconfigure the identity of the nation. Chapter Two then concentrated on counter-hegemonic discourses in Britain and America between 1936 and 1956 and on groups that formulated a positive identity for marginalised or oppressed communities in Britain and America.

More broadly speaking, the number and variety of American theatrical works produced in London from 1936 to 1956, including those by both commercial and subsidised theatres, indicates an abiding interest in American theatre. Critics as well as audiences often shared this interest. Participatory performance involving the intermingling and democratising of activity in the actor/audience relationship would become a core characteristic of the alternative theatre movement in Britain. The trajectory of American influence on this performance practice in British alternative theatre can be traced from the inaugural April 1936 production of Odets' *Waiting for Lefty* at the London Unity Theatre. The interrelationship of space, stage, audience, actor, and author affect the social and cultural efficacy of a given performance. With regard to this process, as Chapter Two has sought to argue, there was a direct exchange of American performance practices such as the Living Newspaper to Britain during this period. Furthermore, the presence of thousands of American service personnel in Britain during wartime and the popularity of American theatrical genres in Britain after World War II introduced American cultural practices to British audiences. This along with British productions of American plays which pushed the boundaries of acceptable subject matter would lay the groundwork for future American influence on experimental theatre and performance practices in Britain during the period 1956–1980.

The influence of the four major American alternative groups which toured Britain during the 1960s and 1970s (Living Theatre, Open Theatre, La MaMa, and Bread and Puppet) on the landscape of British alternative theatre was also critically important. This influence would serve to broaden the horizons of theatre practice in Britain and its engagement with British society. Several anti-Vietnam war protest marches took place during this period, many of which could be argued to involve a certain level of theatricality and included the influence of theatre groups. In a more conventional sense perhaps Peter Brook's production of *US* at the Aldwych Theatre in 1966 was also indicative of this influence.

Jim Haynes from Louisiana was a key founder of the Traverse Theatre in Edinburgh in 1963 and the Arts Lab on Drury Lane in 1967. Experimental venues were immensely important catalysts for change and exemplified innovation on both a technical and aesthetic level. In Edinburgh at the time that the Traverse was formed there was a longing for a permanent home for the excitement and the experimental work of the Festival to be extended throughout the year and this was the basis on which the Traverse Theatre and Gallery were founded. However, Haynes's influence ensured that his legacy as well as that of the Traverse would reach far beyond Edinburgh. This was quickly recognised and can be seen by Harold Hobson's statement, cited earlier, regarding the significance to theatre internationally when Haynes announced that he would leave the Traverse.

The Traverse Theatre in itself was one of the most important sub-cultural developments of its time and without Haynes, it is arguable, it would not have had the wider role, importance, or impact it developed. Yet, Haynes's influence reached far wider after he left the Traverse. Many of those he influenced and supported remain key contributors to alternative British theatre even to this day. As discussed in Chapter Four of this book, many identify the Drury Lane Arts Lab as the very birthplace of the alternative theatre movement in Britain. The Drury Lane Arts Lab was similar to the Traverse in that Haynes brought together at it a wide variety of activities including theatre, music, poetry, and visual art. Perhaps most importantly, it was a space which created an intersection between ideas and creative individuals. As he brought these elements together Haynes generated new personal associations, collaborations, and new forms of creative output.

The focus of Chapter Five was the impact and influence of Charles Marowitz's theatre practice on alternative theatre in Britain during his London period. Marowitz reinvigorated classics by rigorously bending and stretching masterpieces in the form of free adaptations and collages. Controversies associated with Marowitz affected the parameters of censorship, both official and unofficial, in Britain before and after the Theatres Act of 1968. This chapter also proposed that the life and career of Charles Marowitz during his time in Britain did not occur in isolation but within a complex fabric of associations with a wide range of individuals, institutions, and communities. During his British period from 1956 to 1980 his theatre practice and criticism were influential in injecting radical creativity into British theatre. Marowitz's British period 1956–1980 was the prime period of his artistic and intellectual vitality. By analysing the events in his career during this period this study has endeavoured to arrive at a new perspective on this important figure in contemporary theatre.

Chapter Six described how Nancy Meckler and her company Freehold were among the first to utilise the Drury Lane Arts Lab. Meckler moved to London on a permanent basis in April 1968 after working at the La MaMa Plexus in New York. Meckler and her company Freehold were pioneers in Britain, using the body rather than words and conventional literary forms as their primary means of expression (Chambers 1980:106). And as Chapter Six has argued, Freehold would help to introduce 'physical theatre', in a post-Brechtian sense to the British theatrical landscape and introduce a new kind of dramaturgy based on the physicalisation of language. Meckler's other major contribution was in elevating the status of women as directors, and as the primary focus of theatre and performance pieces. Meckler's early career in Britain can also be seen within the context of a generational shift whose energy coalesced in Britain and America largely around the issue of Civil Rights, Women's Rights, and a reaction to American involvement in Vietnam.

Chapter Seven has described how Ed Berman and his company Inter-Action Productions were extremely influential in pioneering unconventional modes of community performance in unconventional locations for non-traditional theatre going audiences. Berman began as a playwright and in 1968 started the first permanent lunchtime theatre in the Britain. Over the next decade the company would be responsible for an extremely prolific range of community arts and professional theatre activities in dozens of venues.

This included the activities of the British American Repertory Company. As mentioned in Chapter Seven the British American Repertory Company was the first joint company approved by both Equity unions in both countries and was designed for non-star actors and stage staff. Berman set up the British-American theatre company creating an exchange of actors and stage managers and the company was hosted by both nations' embassies on either side of the Atlantic. They performed *Dirty Linen* and *Newfoundland* and *Dogg's Hamlet Cahoots Macbeth* which Tom Stoppard had developed with other plays for Berman's theatres.

Further, as described in Chapter Seven Berman's contribution to the British alternative theatre 1956–1980 also included introducing the work of a wide variety of new playwrights, actors, and directors, many of whom went on to great prominence. Berman expanded the diversity of voices represented through his seasons at the Almost Free Theatre which then inspired the creation of many of the theatre groups which participated in the identity-based theatre of the 1970s and 1980s. With his lunchtime theatre, the Fun Art Bus and other initiatives he made theatre available to new audiences and bridged the boundary between the daily life of communities and art. Finally, much of Berman's work was socially and politically active and with the city farms initiative he introduced a new form of environmentalism to British society. His lasting contribution to alternative theatre in Britain, however, lies mainly in the large number of companies and artists whose futures were founded on his open-minded encouragement and producing skills at Inter-Action, his conception of the need for inclusiveness, of working across established social, cultural, sexual, and gender boundaries and his vision of the arts as central to community feeling and health.

Conclusion

Several sources have pointed out that in Britain with subsidised theatre, alternative practices get absorbed very quickly (Meckler, 2012). After World War II, Britain was faced with austerity and was socially conservative. The population wanted to feel safe and secure and for their children to grow up in an ideal structured environment. During the 1950s America made up six percent of the global population but at the same time was responsible for fifty percent of global manufacturing and industry. This unprecedented economic growth in part is why what we now refer to as youth culture started in America. America was a materialist culture in the late 1950s and early 1960s.

The community of young American expatriates included, besides such highly influential figures as Jim Haynes, Charles Marowitz, Ed Berman, and Nancy Meckler, other important figures like Michael Rudman, Bernard Pomerance, Jack Henry Moore, Walter Donohue, and Mike Alfreds who have been mentioned in passing. They all knew each other and were all working on and shaping the Fringe. In addition, *Stages in the Revolution* (1980) along with other theatre scholarship produced by the late American editor and critic Catherine Itzin (*The Alternative Theatre Directory, Theatre Quarterly*) can be seen as evidence that American influence on the alternative theatre movement in Britain (1956–1980) also reached the level of scholarly exchange and historicising. In addition to the individual and collective impetus of the people and groups discussed in this book there was also the background context of two important changes influencing British culture and society. One was a shift in power and influence to the United States as a consequence of changes brought about by World War II. The second was a generational shift both within British theatre and society more generally which can be dated from 1956.

Young Britons found American culture exciting. It was a youth culture and it represented casual living. At the time the Living Theatre first toured through Europe in 1964, Britain had nothing like it. Nobody was doing that sort of practice and there was a certain affinity with American culture, because American culture was seen as different, exciting, and inventive. America had Andy Warhol and artists such as Robert Rauschenberg and Jim Dine. From outside the world of theatre as traditionally defined came the influence of the 'Happening' as pioneered in the 1950s by such American figures as Allan Kaprow and Jim Dine from the visual arts and John Cage from music which incorporated notions of indeterminacy and improvisation.

Yet, there is even a larger discussion to be had on the topic of American influence on British Theatre. There have been a number of studies of post-war British theatre as well as the alternative theatre movement in Britain including Andrew Davies' *Other Theatres* (1987), Baz Kershaw's *The Politics of Performance* (1992), and Dominic Shellard's *British Theatre Since the War* (1999). However, these studies tend to address the influence of French theatre or indigenous developments but do not examine American influence in detail. This study has contributed to the understanding of the forces which have shaped contemporary British theatre by addressing the existing gap in theatre scholarship.

It is also important, however, to take into account that America also depends on Britain in important ways and that this might be the subject of a different book. Joseph Papp, for example, was an important advocate for free public theatre and established the New York Shakespeare Festival Public Theatre in 1967 with the intention of emulating the London branch of the Royal Shakespeare Company in putting on contemporary productions aimed at an audience comprised of a large cross-section of society. The festival opened on 29 October 1967 with *American Tribal Love-Rock Musical*.

The production moved to a nightclub, then was completely restructured by former Cafe La MaMa director Tom O'Horgan and transferred to Broadway as *Hair*. Papp did not prioritise pleasing conventional middle-class Broadway audiences with his work but rather he was interested in connecting with the younger generation who were concerned with contemporary issues and changing society. Britain offered an example of the way in which theatrical innovation advanced across a broad front in the new civic theatres which were essentially a legacy of the war.

What the groups and individuals outlined in this study did was to engender an idealism in which a large number of people, many of whom were young and impressionable, responded. It may have been naive but there was perhaps something liberating and constructive about its energy. It may have been simplistic but it served as a useful corrective to the cynicism inherited from the previous generation. Such a movement dealt in grand generalisations about human life and how people should try and live with one another. It elevated social debate by addressing fundamental issues and how spirituality could be returned to a world that had become intensely materialistic. The younger generation thought that the way to make revolution work was to change the interaction between individuals and to question the bedrock values which produced the status quo. It is the intellectual vestiges of this period which continue to influence contemporary behaviour both private and public (Marwick 1998). The American influences outlined in this book were core to this process.

Abbrevations

BLSA	British Library Sound Archive
DWIC	David Weinberg Interview Collection
NMC	Nancy Meckler Collection
RDA	Richard Demarco Archive
UH	Unfinished Histories

Bibliography

Adorno, Theodor and Max Horkheimer. *The Culture Industry: Enlightenment as Mass Deception*, in *Dialectics of Enlightenment*, trans. J. Cumming, New York: Herder and Herder, 1972.

Anderson, Benedict. *Imagined Communities: Reflections on the Origin and Spread of Nationalism*, London: Verso Books, 2006.

Ansorge, Peter. *Disrupting the Spectacle: Five Years of Experimental & Fringe Theatre in Britain*, London: Pitman Publishing, 1975.

Archer, William. *The Old Drama and the New: An Essay in Re-Evaluation*, London: Dodd, Mead & Co., 1923.

Aronson, Arnold. *American Avant-Garde Theatre: A History*, London & New York: Routledge, 2000.

Artaud, Antonin. *Artaud: Selected Writings*, (edited by Susan Sontag) Berkeley & Los Angeles: University of California Press, 1988.

Barker, Clive. *Theatre Games: A New Approach To Drama Training*, London: Eyre Methuen Ltd, 1977.

Barthes, Roland. *The Death of the Author*, in *Image-Music-Text*, trans. S. Heath, New York: Hill and Wang, 1977.

Bottoms, Stephen. *Playing Underground: A Critical History of the 1960's off-off-Broadway Movement*, Ann Arbor: University of Michigan, 2004.

Brecht, Stephan. *The Bread and Puppet Theatre*, (Volumes One and Two) London: Methuen, 1988.

Brook, Peter. *The Shifting Point: 40 Years of Theatrical Exploration 1946–1987*, London: Methuen Drama, 1987.

Brown, Lorraine and John O'Connor (eds.) *The Federal Theatre Project*, London: Eyre Methuen Ltd, 1980.

Burns, Elizabeth. *Theatricality: A Study of Convention in Theatre and in Social Life*, New York and London: Harper and Row, 1972.

Chambers, Colin. *Inside the Royal Shakespeare Company*, London: Routledge, 2004.

---*The Story of Unity Theatre*, London: Lawrence & Wishart, 1989.

---Other Spaces: New Theatre and the RSC, London: Eyre Methuen Ltd, 1980.

Chambers, Colin and Mike Prior. *Playwrights' Progress: Patterns of Postwar British Drama*, Oxford: Amber Lane Press Ltd, 1987.

Chinoy, Helen Krich, and Toby Cole (eds.) *Actors on Acting*, New York: Crown Publishing, Inc., 1970.

Clarke, Peter. *The Last Thousand Days of the British Empire: Churchill, Roosevelt, and the Birth of Pax Americana*, New York: Bloomsbury Press, 2008.

Clurman, Harold. *The Fervent Years: The Group Theatre and the Thirties*, New York: Da Capo Press, 1983.

Craig, Sandy, ed., *Dreams and Deconstructions: Alternative Theatre in Britain*, Ambergate & Derbyshire: Amber Lane Press, 1980.

Crespy, David. *Off-Off Broadway Explosion: How Provocative Playwrights of the 1960s Ignited a New American Theater*, New York: Back Stage Books, 2003.

Davies, Andrew. *Other Theatres: the Development of Alternative and Experimental Theatre in Britain*, Totowa, New Jersey: Barnes and Noble, 1987.

Derrida, Jacques. *Writing and Difference*, London: Routledge, 2001.

Dunleavy, Patrick. *Authoring a PhD: How to Plan, Draft, Write & Finish a Doctorial Thesis or Dissertation*, London: Palgrave Macmillan, 2003.

Esslin, Martin. *The Theatre of the Absurd*, London: Pelican Books, 1968.

Greenblatt, Stephen. *Shakespearean Negotiations*, Berkeley: University of California Press, 1988.

Goffman, Erving. *The Presentation of Self in Everyday Life*, New York: Anchor Books, 1959.

Hall, Peter. *The Autobiography of Peter Hall: Making an Exhibition of Myself*, London: Sinclair-Stevenson, 1993.

Haynes, Jim. *In Praise of Joy: White-Washing Fences*, Mosaic Press, 2005.

---*Thanks for Coming*, London: Faber & Faber, 1984.

Hewison, Robert. *Too Much: Art & Society in the Sixties 1960–1975*, London: Methuen, 1986.

Itzin, Catherine. (ed.) *Alternative Theatre Handbook*, London: TQ Publications Ltd, 1976.

---*Stages in the Revolution: Political Theatre in Britain Since 1968*, London: Eyre Methuen Ltd, 1980.

Johnson, Jonathan. *Good Hair Days: A Personal Journey with the American Tribal Love-Rock Musical Hair*, New York: iUniverse, Inc., 2004.

Kershaw, Baz. ed., *The Cambridge History of British Theatre (Volume 3)*, Cambridge & New York: Cambridge University Press, 2004.

---*The Politics of Performance: Radical Theatre as Cultural Intervention*, London & New York: Routledge, 1992.

---*The Radical in Performance: Between Brecht and Baudrillard*, London & New York: Routledge, 1999.

Kirby, Michael. *Happenings*, New York: Dutton, 1965.

Kitchen, Laurence. *Mid-Century Drama*, London: Faber, 1962.

Kumar, Ranjit. *Research Methodology*, London: SAGE Publications Ltd. 2005.

Kynaston, David. *Modernity Britain: 1957–1962*, New York & London: Bloomsbury, 2015.

Lane, John. *Arts Centres: Every Town Should Have One*, London: Paul Elek Ltd, 1978.

Marowitz, Charles. *The Act of Being: Towards a Theory of Acting*, New York: Secker & Warburg, 1978.

---*Burnt Bridges: A Souvenir of the Swinging Sixties & Beyond*, London: Hodder & Stoughton, 1990.

---*Confessions of a Counterfeit Critic: A London Theatre Notebook 1958–1971*, London: Eyre Methuen Ltd, 1973.

---*The Encore Reader: A Chronicle of the New Drama*, (edited with Tom Milne & Owen Hale) London: Eyre Methuen, 1965.

---*The Method as Means-An Acting Survey*, London: H. Jenkins, 1961.

---*The Other Chekhov: A Biography of Michael Chekhov, the Legendary Actor, Director & Theorist*, New York & London: Applause Theatre & Cinema Books, 2004.

---*The Other Way: An Alternative Approach to Acting & Directing*, New York & London: Applause Books, 1998.

---*Prospero's Staff*, Bloomington & Indianapolis: Indiana University Press, 1986.

---*Recycling Shakespeare*, London: Macmillan Education, 1991.

---*Roar of the Canon: Kott & Marowitz on Shakespeare*, New York & London: Applause Theatre & Cinema Books, 2001.

---*Stage Dust: A Critic's Cultural Scrapbook from the 1990's*, Lanham MD: Scarecrow Press, 2001.

---*Stanislavsky & the Method*, New York: Citadel Press, 1964.

---*Theatre at Work: Playwrights & Productions in the Modern British Theatre*. A Collection of Interviews & Essays, (edited with Simon Trussler) London: Hill & Wang, 1968.

Marshall, Norman. *The Other Theatre*, London: John Lehmann Ltd, 1947.

Marwick, Arthur. *The Sixties: Cultural Revolution in Britain, France, Italy and the United States, c.1958–c.1974*, Oxford and New York: Oxford University Press, 1998.

Mason, Jeffrey and Ellen Gainor, (eds.) *Performing America: Cultural Nationalism in American Theater*, Ann Arbor: University of Michigan Press, 1999.

McMillan, Joyce. *The Traverse Theatre Story 1963–1988*, London: Methuen Drama, 1988.

Meserve, Walter. *An Outline History of American Drama*, Totowa, New Jersey: Littlefield, Adams and Co., 1965.

Miles, Barry. *London Calling: A Countercultural History of London Since 1945*, London: Atlantic Books, 2010.

Miller, Arthur. *Timebends: A Life*, London: Methuen, 1987.

Moffat, Alistair. *The Edinburgh Fringe*, London & Edinburgh: Cassell Ltd, 1978.

Nuttall, Jeff. *Bomb Culture*, London: Paladin, 1968.

Rebellato, Dan. *1956 and All That: The Making of Modern British Drama*, London & New York: Routledge, 1999.

Rees, Roland. *Fringe First: Pioneers of Fringe Theatre on Record*, London: Oberon Books Limited, 1992.

Reynolds, David. *Rich Relations: The American Occupation of Britain, 1942–1945*, New York: Random House, 1995.

Sampson, Anthony. *Anatomy of Britain*, New York & Evanston: Harper & Row, 1962.

Schiele, Jinnie. *Off-Centre Stages: Fringe Theatre at the Open Space and the Round House 1968–1983*, University of Hertfordshire Press & Society for Theatre Research, 2005.

Selden, Raman, Peter Widdowson and Peter Brooker. *A Reader's Guide to Contemporary Literary Theory*, Harlow, Essex: Prentice Hall, 1997.

Shaw, George Bernard. *The Quintessence of Ibsenism,* London: Forgotten Books, 2010.

Shellard, Dominic. *British Theatre Since the War,* New Haven & London: Yale University Press, 1999.

Stafford-Clark, Max and Philip Roberts. *Taking Stock: The Theatre of Max Stafford-Clark,* London: Nick Hern Books, 2007.

Stanley, William. *Broadway in the West End: An Index of Reviews of American Theatre in London, 1950–1975,* London: Greenwood Press, 1978.

Tynan, Kenneth. *A View of the English Stage 1944–1963,* London: Davis-Poynter Limited, 1975.

--- *Kenneth Tynan Letters,* (edited by Kathleen Tynan) London: Weidenfeld & Nicolson, 1994.

--- *Kenneth Tynan Theatre Writings,* (selected & edited by Dominic Shellard), London: Nick Hern Books, 2007.

Tytell, John. *The Living Theatre: Art, Exile and Outrage,* London: Methuen Drama, 1997.

Walker, Daniel. *Rights in Conflict: Convention Week in Chicago, August 25–29, 1968,* New York: E.P. Dutton, 1968.

Wardle, Irving. *Theatre Criticism,* London: Routledge, 1992.

---*The Theatres of George Devine,* London: Jonathan Cape, 1978.

Williams, Raymond. *Drama from Ibsen to Brecht,* London: Penguin Books Ltd, 1968.

Wintle, Justin. *The Fun Art Bus, An Inter-Action Project by Ed Berman,* London: Eyre Methuen Ltd, 1973.

Wollman, Elizabeth. *The Theatre Will Rock: A History of the Rock Musical from Hair to Hedwig,* Ann Arbor: University of Michigan Press, 2006.

Wright, Adrian. *West End Broadway: The Golden Age of the American Musical in London,* Woodbridge UK: The Boydell Press, 2012.

Archives

BRITISH LIBRARY SOUND ARCHIVE
96 Euston Road, London NW1 2DB, United Kingdom
Email: Customer-Services@bl.uk
Switchboard: +44 (0)330 333 1144
Customer Services: +44 (0)1937 546060
(http://sounds.bl.uk: Theatre Archive Project)
Interviewee: Anthony Field
Date: 14 March 2007
Interviewer: Kate Harris

David Weinberg Interview Collection

33 Shepherds Hill, London N6 5QJ, United Kingdom
Email: davew.48@juno.com
Phone: +44 (0)7903146846

Interviewee: Ian Brown
Date: 2 February 2011
Location: Kingston University
Interviewer: David Weinberg

Interviewee: Colin Chambers
Date: 16 February 2011
Location: Kingston University
Interviewer: David Weinberg

Interviewee: Richard Demarco C.B.E.
Date: 9 May 2011
Location: Edinburgh
Interviewer: David Weinberg

Interviewee: Charles Marowitz
Date: 5 June 2011
Location: Malibu, California
Interviewer: David Weinberg

Interviewee: Jim Haynes
Date: 5 August 2011
Location: London
Interviewer: David Weinberg

Interviewee: Nancy Meckler
Date: 14 January 2012
Location: London
Interviewer: David Weinberg

Nancy Meckler Collection (London)

Email: nanmeck@gmail.com

Richard Demarco Archive

11 Upper Cramond Court,Edinburgh EH4 6RQ, United Kingdom
Email: richard@richarddemarco.org
Phone: +44 (0)77489 61315

Unfinished Histories

Room 15, St Margaret's House Settlement, 21 Old Ford Road, London E2 9PL United Kingdom
Email: contact@unfinishedhistories.com
Phone: +44 (0)20 3659 5678

(http://www.unfinishedhistories.com/interviews/interviewees/jim-haynes/)
Interviewee: Jim Haynes
Date: 31 September 2009
Location: Paris
Interviewer: Susan Croft
Technician: Jessica Higgs

(http://www.unfinishedhistories.com/interviews/interviewees/max-stafford-clark/)
Interviewee: Max Stafford-Clark
Date: 8 December 2009
Location: North London
Interviewer: Carole Woddis

(http://www.unfinishedhistories.com/interviews/interviewees/roland-rees/)
Interviewee: Roland Rees
Date: 10 December 2009, 11 January 2010 and 5 April 2011
Location: Peckham, London
Interviewer: Susan Croft
Recorded by: Jessica Higgs
© Roland Rees and In Tandem TC (Intantc@aol.com)

(http://www.unfinishedhistories.com/interviews/interviewees/ed-berman/)
Interviewee: Ed Berman
Date: 4th December 2010 and 13th February 2011
Location: Isle of Dogs, London
Interviewer: Susan Croft
Recorded by: Jessica Higgs
© ED Berman and In Tandem TC (Intantc@aol.com)

(http://www.unfinishedhistories.com/interviews/interviewees/beth-porter/)
Interviewee: Beth Porter
Date & place: 24 February 2011, Frant, Sussex
Interviewer: Susan Croft
Recorded by: Jessica Higgs
© Beth Porter and In Tandem TC (Intantc@aol.com)

Unfinished Histories Exhibition Event
Speaker: Dr Susan Croft
Date: 8 April 2014
Location: Holborn Library

Journal & Newspaper Articles

Anon. 'Catherine Itzin, Obituary', *Guardian,* 12 April 2010.

Anon. 'Jeff Nuttall, Obituary', *Guardian,* 11 January 2004.

Billington, Michael. 'United Stages of America', *Guardian,* 3 December 2008, (front section) p.32.

Ellis, Samantha. '*Macbeth,* London, May 1969: Three Thanes of Cawdor and a see-through nightie put Marowitz's *Macbeth* on the map, May 20 1969', *Guardian,* 19 November 2003, (arts section).

Marowitz, Charles. 'Artaud at Rodez,' *Theatre Quarterly,* 2 (1972), 58–62

---'The Critic as Artist,' *Plays and Players,* (October 1971), 64–72

---'The Marowitz Macbeth', *Theatre Quarterly,* 1 (1971), no. 3 47–49

---'An Open Letter to the Becks, *Plays & Players* (June, 1969)

Shank, Theodore. 'Collective Creation', *The Drama Review,* 16 (1972), no. 2, 3–31

Wardle, Irving. 'The "Arts Lab Explosion"', *The Times,* 21 December 1968, (Theatre section)

--- 'The British Sixties', *Performance,* Volume 1 Number 1, December 1971.

Younge, Gary. 'Pop, Sex & Civil rights: Was 1963 the start of modern life?' *Guardian,* 7 May 2013, (G2 section) p. 12.

Play Texts

Albee, Edward. *The American Dream,* London: Jonathan Cape, 1962.

Albee, Edward. *The Collected Plays of Edward Albee: Volume 1 1958–1965,* New York: Overlook Press, 2004.

---*The Collected Plays of Edward Albee: 1966–1977,* New York: Overlook Press, 2004.

Anderson, Robert. *Tea and Sympathy*, New York: Random House Inc., 1953.

Andreyev, Leonid. *He Who Gets Slapped*, Charleston SC: Nabu Press, 2010.

Arden, Jane. *Vagina Rex and the Gas Oven*, London: Calder & Boyars Ltd, 1971.

Bellow, Saul. *The Bellow Plays*, in *The Open Space Play*, London: Penguin Books, 1974.

Chayefsky, Paddy. *The Latent Heterosexual*, New York: Random House, 1967.

Crowley, Mart. *The Boys in the Band*, New York: Samuel French, Inc., 2010.

Feiffer, Jules. *Crawling Arnold*, New York: Dramatis Play Service, Inc., 1998.

Foster, Paul. *Tom Paine*, London: Calder & Boyars, 1967.

Garson, Barbara. *Macbird*, London: Penguin, 1967.

Gelber, Jack. *The Connection*, New York: Grove Press, 1960.

Genet, Jean. *The Blacks*, New York: Grove Press, 1994.

Gogol, Nikolai V. *Marriage*, in *Gogol Three Plays*, London: Methuen, 1999.

Guare, John. *Muzeeka*, New York: Dramatists Play Service, Inc., 1968.

Hansberry, Lorraine. *A Raisin in the Sun*, New York: Knopf Doubleday Publishing Group, 2011.

Haynes, Jim, ed. *Traverse Plays*, London: Penguin Books Ltd, 1966.

Herbert, John. *Fortune and Men's Eyes*, in *Open Space Plays*, London: Penguin Books, 1974.

Ibsen, Henrick. *Four Great Plays by Henrick Ibsen*, New York: Bantam Books, 1959.

Kopit, Arthur. *Indians*, New York: Hill and Wang, 1969.

Marowitz, Charles. *Artaud at Rodez,* London: Marion Boyars Publishers Ltd, 1977.

---*Boulevard Comedies: Free Adaptations of Becque, Feydeu & Moliere,* Ann Arbor: University of Michigan Press, 2000

---*Four American Plays,* London: Penguin Books, 1970.

---*The Marowitz Shakespeare: Adaptations & Collages of Hamlet, Macbeth, The Taming of the Shrew, Measure for Measure and the Merchant of Venice,* New York & London: Marion Boyars Publishers Ltd, 1978.

---*New American Drama,* (Contributor) London: Penguin Books, 1973.

---*Off-Broadway Plays,* Volumes 1 & 2 (editor) London: Penguin Books, 1970 & 1972.

---*Open Space Plays,* (editor) London: Penguin Books, 1974.

---*Potboilers: Three Black Comedies,* New York & London: Marion Boyars Publishers Ltd, 1986.

---*Sex Wars: Free Adaptations of Ibsen & Strindberg,* Boston & London: Marion Boyers Ltd, 1982.

McNally, Terence. *Sweet Eros,* in *Off-Broadway Plays 2,* Middlesex UK: Harmondsworth, 1972.

Miller, Arthur. *The Man Who Had All the Luck,* London: Methuen Drama, 2008.

---*A View from the Bridge,* New York: Penguin Classics, 2010.

Moliere. *The Miser & George Dandin,* New York: Applause, 2000.

Odets, Clifford. *Waiting for Lefty,* New York: Dramatists Play Service, Inc., 1935.

Orton, Joe *Loot,* London: Methuen Drama, 2013.

Osborne, John. *Look Back in Anger,* New York: Penguin, 1982.

Owens, Rochelle. *Futz & What Came After,* New York: Random House, 1968.

Picasso, Pablo. (trans. R. Penrose) *The Four Little Girls,* London: Calder Publications Ltd, 1970.

Ragni, Gerome, and James Rado. *Hair: The American Tribal Love-Rock Musical,* New York: Pocket Books, 1969.

Steinbeck, John. *Of Mice and Men,* New York: Dramatis Play Service, Inc., 1937.

Stoppard, Tom. *After Magritte,* London: Faber and Faber, 1975.

---*Dirty Linen & New-Found-Land,* London: Faber and Faber Limited, 1976.

---*Dogg's Hamlet, Cohoot's Macbeth,* London: Faber and Faber, 1980.

Terry, Megan. *Viet-Rock,* New York: Simon & Schuster, 1967.

Van Itallie, Jean-Claude. *America Hurrah: And Other Plays, The Serpent, A Fable, The Hunter and the Bird, Almost Like Being ,* New York: Grove Press, Inc., 1978.

Vidal, Gore. *Visit to a Small Planet,* New York: Dramatis Play Service, Inc., 1958.

Wardle, Irving. *The Houseboy,* in *Open Space Plays,* London: Penguin Books, 1974.

Weiss, Peter. *The Marat/Sade,* New York: Pocket Books, 1968.

Williams, Tennessee. *Cat on a Hot Tin Roof,* New York: New Directions Books, 1955.

--- *A Streetcar Named Desire,* New York: Dramatists Play Service, Inc., 1947.

--- *This Property is Condemned,* New York: New Directions, 1966.

Yankowitz, Susan. *Terminal,* in *Three Works by the Open Theatre,* New York: Drama Book Specialists, 1974.

ibidem-Verlag / *ibidem* Press
Melchiorstr. 15
70439 Stuttgart
Germany

ibidem@ibidem.eu
ibidem.eu